Riders on the Earth

Riders on the Earth

Essays and Recollections

by

Archibald MacLeish

Houghton Mifflin Company Boston

1978

Acknowledgments and permissions
information follow the text,
beginning on page 155.

Library of Congress Cataloging in Publication Data

MacLeish, Archibald, 1892–
    Riders on the Earth.

    Includes index.
    I. Title.
PS3525.A27R5   811'.5'2   [B]   77-27015
ISBN 0-395-26382-4

Printed in the United States of America

W 10 9 8 7 6 5 4 3 2 1

Foreword

THE ARTICLES, essays, reflections, memoirs collected in this book were written, most of them, in the late sixties and early seventies. It was a bad time in the history of the Republic — a bad time in the chronicles of mankind — but some of these pieces permit themselves, notwithstanding, a degree of hope and require, therefore, explanation: a reminder, in any case, that a bad time may be a beginning rather than an end. If a generation is bold enough to face up to the truth about its troubles — bold enough to accept the truth, grow angry, rage — it may arrive at a state of honest indignation, violent revulsion against a dirty past, which will renew the future and give its aspirations hope.

Certainly something of that kind happened to us at the close of the Nixon epoch. We not only faced up to the incredible facts about the Nixon White House but, having learned to endure the taste of truth, we developed a hunger for it, a relish for the anger it aroused, and, eventually, a passionate determination that the great human hope which had been threatened by that corruption should not be destroyed. The Republic would prove its fundamental proposition that men are capable of governing themselves in spite of everything, lying presidents included.

And other things were, of course, included. Not only did we find ourselves engaged in a war we had never declared and about which we were constantly deceived — a war over which we had little or no control — but we discovered, at more or less the same time, that our power to govern ourselves had been paralyzed in other and more subtle ways. Fundamental decisions were being made, not by us but for us, and not only by dishonest officials but by something called science or technology or progress which increasingly, year by year, did whatever could be done *because* it could be done and not because it was humanly needed or even humanly desirable. Weapons became more and more murderously destructive until they were capable of destroying not only an enemy but the planet itself. Businesses and governments became computerized and automatic to such a point that their bureaucracies turned into machines and the human beings they dealt with into statistics. Human reason which had once attempted to explain the world and plan its future fell into disrepute and even literature itself, terrified by the insanities around it, took refuge in a childish dream of the absurdity of everything.

But even this deeper sense of helplessness and impotence was redeemed by our revulsion to the Nixon administration. If the suffocating frustration of the Vietnam War could be faced, and the corruption of the White House exposed, and an honest president installed in place of that other, then conceivably we could talk at last about the tyranny of "progress" and the mechanization of life and the spiritual degradation of the great Republic. And we did. Not for a long time has there been as angry a reassessment of our underlying beliefs as there has been in the last few years. A new American Nobel laureate in letters called upon his fellow writers to return from the peripheries to the human center. Newspaper editors from one end of the country to the other published editorials about our old revolutionary commitment to human rights, pro and con. Distinguished scientists argued openly against feckless reverence for a science which suspends all judgments of the doubtful miracles it works. Ordinary citizens protested so passionately against the mechanized bureaucracies of government and of monster corporations that the computer and its superhuman skills became an issue in elections. And common writers like myself discovered that they could not understand their time without attempting to understand these grievances and the new and opening hope toward which they turned.

For this difficult time of ours has hopes not known before — or, more precisely, hopes long known but now, because we have faced these difficulties, more believable than once they were. It is for that reason I have used as epigraph to this book a little piece I wrote for the *New York Times* when the Apollo mission of 1968 returned from space with that famous photograph of our earth as seen from out beyond the moon: the photograph which gave mankind its first understanding of its actual situation; riders on the earth together, brothers on that bright loveliness in the unending night — brothers who *see* now they are truly brothers.

Contents

CONTENTS

Bubble of Blue Air

O UR CONCEPTION of ourselves and of each other has always depended on our image of the earth.

When the earth was the World — all the world there was — and the stars were lights in Dante's Heaven, and the ground beneath our feet roofed Hell, we saw ourselves as creatures at the center of the universe, the sole particular concern of God.

And when, centuries later, the earth was no longer the world but a small, wet, spinning planet in the solar system of a minor star off at the edge of an inconsiderable galaxy in the vastnesses of space — when Dante's Heaven foundered and there was no Hell — no Hell, at least, beneath our feet — men began to see themselves not as God-directed actors in the solemn paces of a noble play, but rather as the victims of an idiotic farce where all the rest were victims also and multitudes had perished without meaning.

Now, in this latest generation of mankind, the image may have altered once again. For the first time in all of time men have seen the earth with their own eyes — seen the whole earth in the vast void as even Dante never dreamed of seeing it — seen what whimpering victims could not guess a man might see.

The medieval notion of the earth put man at the center of everything. The scientific notion put him nowhere: beyond the range of sense or reason, lost in absurdity and death. This latest notion may have other consequences. Formed as it was in the eyes of heroic voyagers who were also men, it may remake our lost conception of ourselves. No longer the preposterous player at the center of an unreal stage — no longer that degraded and degrading victim off at the verges of reality and blind with blood — man may discover what he really is.

To see the earth as we now see it, small and blue and beautiful in that eternal silence where it floats, is to see ourselves as riders on the earth together, brothers on that bright loveliness in the unending night — brothers who *see* now they are truly brothers.

PART I

Six Essays

1

Return from the Excursion

ALL IT TAKES to strip an emperor naked is a small boy who dares to tell him that he has no clothes. So says the fable and it is true fable — as every generation learns — true not only of emperors but of every accepted pomposity on earth, and not only of the voices of small boys, but of every voice still capable of innocence and truth, Nobel laureates included.

Saul Bellow, our latest laureate in letters, demonstrated that at Stockholm in December 1976 when he called on his fellow writers to "return from the peripheries." To tell the writers of the world to return from the peripheries to the center, to "the main human enterprise," is, in effect, to tell them that they are not at the center now. Indeed, Saul Bellow told them so precisely in so many words: "We do not, we writers, represent mankind adequately." We do not satisfy the "immense painful longing" of mankind . . . It would be difficult, I think, to put the accusation more comprehensively. But Bellow's words not only draw the indictment; they also identify the suspect. They strip the trousers from one of the most pompous propositions of our time.

I refer, of course, to the proposition which drove the art of letters from the human center to the peripheral islands, the peninsulas of ice, some thirty years ago: the notion propagated, largely in France, after the Second World War, that Aristotle had somehow died in that great disaster, and that truth to life was no longer the criterion of art because life was no longer the criterion of anything — life had been found out at last — life was absurd.

For decades after the Second World War this tremendous discovery was paraded up and down to the applause of undergraduates, American and other, and not a voice was raised to call it naked, not a finger pointed. Even the most intelligent critics held their tongues. I remember one of the best of them reporting some years back that the novelists she most admired seemed to be addicted to what she called "the literature of extreme situations" — sexual aberrations, madness in various forms, drugs, suicide (always suicide) and the extraneous generally — having said which she concluded with the statement that the reason for this addiction was "not apparent" and left it at that.

Not so Saul Bellow at Stockholm. Saul Bellow, though he did not mention Aristotle's name or recall his words — only those of Conrad and of Proust — refused to walk across the corpse as though it were not there. He reminded his fellow writers that the human center still existed and was still the center and that the peripheries were what they always had been: peripheries; fogbanks off at sea.

One wonders, now the words have been said, how this parading emperor kept his dignity so long. Who pesuaded us of the Absurd?

There have been discoveries about the human condition in the past which were truly discoveries — realizations by whole generations of humankind that life was not what men had once supposed it. Was the Absurd a realization of this kind? Was it suddenly true for entire nations, for humankind, that life is, in its nature, its condition, an absurdity? Or was this another kind of event altogether: not an intuition of the common human heart, not a perception of the brooding arts, but a thesis composed by the ideologues, an intellectual theory? Not, in other words, a discovery at all — not even a voyage to sea? A mere excursion to the lighthouse?

I, for my part, think it was. I think, further, that the greatest propagator of the Absurd, that admirable man and enchanting writer, Camus, never believed in it. It is true, of course, that Camus wrote *The Stranger*, which was published, we have been told, to prove that "the inevitability of death destroys all values." But Camus also wrote: "The great artist is first and foremost a man who has had a great experience of life." How is a man, even a great artist, to have a great experience of absurdity? And then there are the *Notebooks*. Everyone remembers the docker with the broken leg:

> In the café he tells me the story of his life. The others have gone. Six glasses stand on the table. He lived alone in a small house in the suburbs, going home only in the evening to do the cooking. A dog, a tom and a female cat, six kittens which the cat cannot feed. They die one by one. Every evening a stiff dead body and filth. Two smells: death and urine mingling together. On the last evening (he stretches his arms across the table wider and wider apart, slowly and gently pushing the glasses toward the edge) the last kitten died. But the mother had eaten half of it — half a cat left, as you might say. And still all

the filth. The wind howling around the house. A piano in the far distance. He sat in the middle of these ruins and wretchedness. And the whole meaning of the world had suddenly surged up into his mouth. (One by one the glasses fall from the table as he stretches his arms wider and wider apart.) He stayed there for a long time, shaking with a vast, wordless anger, his head in his hands and the thought that he had got to get his dinner ready . . .

But four months later we find Camus saying of a different, a more personal protagonist:

And he went into the water washing off the dark and contorted images left there by the world. Suddenly the rhythm of his muscles brought back to life the smell of his own skin. Perhaps never before had he been so aware of the harmony between himself and the world, of the rhythm linking his movements with the daily course of the sun. Now when the night was overflowing with stars his gestures stood out against the sky's immense and silent face . . .

And always there are the attempted resolutions of these antiphonies: With all my silence I shall protest to the very end . . . It is my revolt which is right, and it must follow this joy which is like a pilgrim on earth, follow it step by step.

And again in an imagined conversation:

It doesn't seem as if this world satisfies you from the way you talk about it.

It doesn't satisfy me because it's going to be taken away from me — or rather it's because it satisfies me too much that I can feel all the horror of losing it.

Return from the Excursion

And again:

The misery and greatness of this world: it offers no truths but only objects for love. Absurdity is king but love saves us from it.

"Absurdity is king but love saves us." Life is absurd — and therefore we must live our own lives — find our own meanings in life — love's meanings. As one reads the *Notebooks* one sees that it is not life which is absurd to Camus but the *idea* of life — the idea of life ending in death — the idea of life with all its happiness and death beyond for answer. Life, life *as* life, is as dear to Camus as it was to Sappho herself to whom "the bright and the beautiful" belonged "to the desire of the sunlight." To attribute to *him* the notion that human existence as such is an absurdity which has no relevance to art, which cannot measure the work of art, to which the work of art need not be referred, is grotesque.

But if Camus is not a witness to the *truth* of the discovery that human life is absurd, who is? One looks in these matters to the poets, "God's spies." The new perceptions, the massive realizations, of an epoch form in its poems: in the *Odes* of Keats, in the *Illuminations* of Rimbaud, in the *Elegies* of Rilke. If it is true that the age we live in has discovered the previously unperceived absurdity of human life — the fundamental meaninglessness of existence — we should look, for traces of that discovery, to the poets of the age. Would we find it?

Would we find it in Frost who lived longest in this time? Frost quarreled with the world, quarreled with it constantly, was prouder, perhaps, of his quarrel with the world than of anything else in his long life. Had *he* discovered its tragic absurdity?

7

Far in the pillared dark
Thrush music went —
Almost like a call to come in
To the dark and lament.

But no, I was out for stars:
I would not come in.
I meant, not even if asked,
And I hadn't been.

Or leave the United States. Go back to Europe where the old sophistication is. Go back to the poets of Europe. This time of ours of which we are so conscious, which we are forever poking and prodding and questioning — as the men of Athens and Rome and Paris and high England never poked and prodded — this time of ours, whatever else it has been, is an age of European poets. Yeats in Britain, Kazantzakis and Seferis in Greece, Guillén and Neruda in the Spanish world, Perse in the French. What is the burden of their song? The discovery of meaninglessness? The expulsion from Eden? The belated realization that human life is absurd in its underlying condition as human life, and that the greatest absurdity, therefore, is to make poems of it — make sense of it in poems?

None of them, and least of all the greatest, preach this sermon. Yeats, that famous praiser of "such men as come/Proud, open-eyed and laughing to the tomb," understands well enough that "all things pass away" but draws a contrary conclusion:

Everything that man esteems
Endures a moment or a day.
Love's pleasure drives his love away,

Return from the Excursion

The painter's brush consumes his dreams.
The herald's cry, the soldier's tread
Exhaust his glory and his might:
Whatever flames upon the night
Man's own resinous heart has fed.

Guillén, whose *Cántico* is one long song of praise, founds his certainty in the wonder of the world, in being:

Even the daisies
Have a kingdom off in the distance,
With some yellow bud or other,
Happy at being a solid form.
. . . .
Will so much beauty spill over?
I want it to spill.
Maybe a slow, useless
Joy is enough . . .

Even Seferis whose vision is darker than the others — Seferis who, like Perse, was statesman as well as poet and lived through the political delusions of the middle century — brings back no vision of a meaningless existence. The sadness of his poems is the sadness not of newly perceived absurdity but of a present which has lost its past, of a meaning which is elsewhere:

What are they after, our souls, traveling
on the decks of decayed ships
crowded in with sallow women and crying babies
unable to forget themselves either with the flying fish
or with the stars that the masts point out at their tips

grated by gramophone records
committed to nonexistent pilgrimages unwillingly,
murmuring broken thoughts from foreign languages?

What are they after, our souls, traveling
on rotten brine-soaked timbers
from harbor to harbor?
. . .
We knew that the islands were beautiful
somewhere round about here where we're groping —
a little nearer or a little farther,
the slightest distance.

And as for Perse, not even the sadness overwhelms:

I saw smiling in the fires of the open sea the great festive
thing: the Sea as celebrated in our dreams, like an Easter of
green grasses and like a feast day that we celebrate,
. . . The drums of nothingness yield to the fifes of light . . .

If you read the great poems of the time you do not find proof of this immense discovery which is supposed to have divorced our age from its trust in life.

Indeed, if you read poems of the time you may find proof of the opposite, proof that our lives, precisely because we die and know we die, are truer to us than they were when we thought we might live forever; proof that the world, precisely because we must lose it, precisely because we cannot understand our loss of it, is inexpressibly ours.

No, the poets, the great poets of our time at least, are not the discoverers of the Absurd. They do not even believe in the

Absurd now that the discovery has been proclaimed. But when have they ever believed in doctrine? And, what is more certain, now that a few years have gone by and we have had an opportunity to grow accustomed to this terrifying word — what is more certain than the fact that the whole notion of the absurdity of life *is* doctrine: a conclusion reached, not by that intense and passionate observation of life of which poetry is capable, of which art is capable, but by a purely intellectual process, by philosophizing and theologizing, by abstracting and deducing, by departing from premises to arrive at the conclusions of those premises?

No one doubts that, in the world of ideas, the inevitability of death makes human effort as pointless as the labor of Sisyphus. But it is not in the world of ideas that life is *lived*. Life is lived for better or worse *in* life, and to a man *in* life his life can no more be absurd than it can be the opposite of absurd, whatever that opposite may be. It *is*. And *he* is, in it. Buckminster Fuller following Whitehead who knew that "the process is the reality," once remarked that "truth is a verb." Life is a verb also. It may be ridiculous to a god observing it but to ourselves who live it, who *are* the verb, the process, the becoming, it cannot be ridiculous. Hateful, yes. Brutal, often. Painful, frequently. Tragic, without doubt. But ridiculous? Only in words. Only on a printed page.

Why then have so many of us accepted this doctrine? Why have great numbers of intellectuals accepted it, founded a whole critical position upon it? — done their considerable best to herd contemporary writing through this crooked gate? Why has a generation of writers removed to the peripheries? Perhaps because so much has changed in this age of change that life itself,

or so we think, must have altered with it. Life *has* changed —
but not in its condition, its reality, *as life*. And not certainly in
its relation to the arts it produces. Aristotle's question is still the
only question to which the arts respond with all their meaning,
all their strength. To fail to ask the arts to be true to life is not
to liberate the arts into a greater freedom but to diminish them,
reduce them to skills and knacks, games and devices — critics'
games.

It was Aristotle's question Saul Bellow put to his fellow
writers at Stockholm when he stood there speaking of the
periphery and the center: "Writers are greatly respected," he
said. "The intelligent public is wonderfully patient with them,
continues to read them and endures disappointment after disappointment after disappointment, waiting to hear from art what
it does not hear from theology, philosophy, social theory, and
what it cannot hear from pure science . . . a broader, more
flexible, fuller, more coherent, more comprehensive account of
what we human beings are, who we are, and what this life is
for."

2
The Revolt of the Diminished Man

R OBERT F ROST had the universe, not the university, in mind
when he wrote his laconic couplet about the secret in the
middle, but the image fits the academic world in crisis as well as
the mysteries of space.

> *We dance round in a ring and suppose,*
> *But the Secret sits in the middle and knows.*

It certainly did in the sixties and so did we. Faculty commit-
tees, state legislatures, alumni associations, police departments,
and all the rest of us whirled in a circle with our favorite sup-
positions — which increasingly tended to roll up into one supposition: that the crisis in the university was really only a student crisis, or, more precisely, a crisis precipitated by a small
minority of students, which would go away if the students
would stop doing whatever it was they were doing or whatever
they planned to do next.

Which, needless to say, was not a wholly irrational supposition. Those who saw a purposeful task force of Harvard students take over University Hall, carry out reluctant deans, break into files, shout down professors, were within their logical rights when they concluded that the occupying students were the cause of the crisis thus created. But the supposition remains a supposition notwithstanding for it does not follow — did not follow at Harvard certainly — that the crisis was a student crisis in the critical sense that it could be ended merely by suppressing the students involved. When the students involved were suppressed at Harvard, the crisis (as at other universities) was not reduced but enlarged. Which suggests, if it suggests anything, that the actual crisis was larger than its particular incidents or their perpetrators.

And there are other familiar facts which look in the same direction; as, for example, the fact that it was only when the general opinion of an entire student generation supported or at least condoned minority disruptions that they could hope to succeed. The notion that the activist tail wagged the huge, indifferent student dog was an illusion. Had a minority of the kind involved at Harvard attempted to bring the university to that famous "grinding halt" in the forties or the fifties, it would have had its trouble for its pains. It succeeded in the sixties for one reason and for one reason only: because the climate of student opinion as a whole had changed in the sixties; because there had been a change in the underlying beliefs, the accepted ideas, of an entire academic generation, or the greater part of it.

To look for the cause of crisis, therefore, is to examine, not the demands of the much discussed minorities but something larger — the changes in belief of the generation to which they belonged. And there at once a paradox appears. The most strik-

14

ing of these changes, far from disturbing the academic world, should and does encourage it. There were, of course, romantics in the new generation who talked of destroying the university as a symbol of a defunct civilization, but the great mass of their contemporaries, however little they sometimes seemed to understand the nature of the university — the vulnerability, fragility even, of that free and open community of minds which a university is — were nevertheless profoundly concerned with the university's well-being and, specifically, its relation to the world and to themselves.

This was a new thing under the academic sun and, in itself, a hopeful thing. Down to the decade of the sixties, demands by any considerable number of American undergraduates for changes in the substance or manner or method or purpose of their instruction were rare indeed. In my day at Yale, back before the First World War, no one concerned himself less with matters of curriculum and teaching and the like than a college undergraduate. We were not, as undergraduates, indifferent to our education, but it never occurred to any of us to think of the curriculum of Yale College as a matter within our concern, or the policies of the university as decisions about which we — we of all creatures living — were entitled to an opinion. Some of my college classmates protested compulsory chapel (largely because of its interference with breakfast), but no one to my knowledge ever protested, even in a letter to the *News*, the pedantic teaching of Shakespeare, from which the college then suffered, or the nonteaching of Karl Marx, who was then on the point of changing the history of the world.

And the same thing was true of the relation between the university and the world outside. We in the class of 1915 spent our senior year in a Yale totally surrounded by the First World War, but we were "inside," and all the rest were "outside," and it was not for us to put the two together — not even for those of us who were to go from New Haven to die on the Marne or in the Argonne under extremely unpleasant circumstances in the most murderous, hypocritical, unnecessary, and generally nasty of all recorded wars. Our deaths, as we came to know, would be our own but not their reasons. When I myself was asked by a corporal in my battery what we were there for — "there" being the second battle of the Marne — I quoted President Wilson: "To make the world safe for democracy."

And the generation which fought the next war twenty years later saw things in much the same way. They too were in a sense observers — observers, in their case, of their own heroism. When the war came they fought it with magnificent courage: no citizen army in history ever fought better than theirs after that brutal North African initiation. But until the war came, while it was still in the agonizing process of becoming, it was somebody else's war — President Roosevelt's, as the *Chicago Tribune* kept insinuating, or Winston Churchill's. "America First" was in part, a campus movement, but the terrible question posed by Adolf Hitler — a question of life or death for thousands of young Americans and very possibly for the Republic itself — was little argued by the undergraduates of 1941. The political aspects of fascism they left to their elders at home and the moral agony to their contemporaries in the French Resistance. They themselves merely fought the war and won it — fought it with a kind of gallant indifference, an almost ironic gallantry, which was, and still remains, the hallmark of that incredible generation and its improbable triumph.

The Revolt of the Diminished Man

It is in this perspective and against this background that the attitudes of the undergraduates of the sixties must be seen. Here, suddenly and almost without warning, was a generation of undergraduates that reversed everything that had gone before, rejected the traditional undergraduate isolation, refused the conventional segregation of the university from the troubled world, and not only accepted for itself but demanded for itself a measure of responsibility for both — for university *and* world, for life as well as for education.

And the question, if we wish to understand this famous crisis, is: Why? Why has this transformation of ideas — metamorphosis more precisely — taken place? Why did the generation of the sixties make itself morally responsible for the war in Vietnam, while the generation of 1917 stood on the Marne quoting Woodrow Wilson and the generation of 1941 smashed the invincible Nazi armor from Normandy to the Rhine without a quotation from anybody? Why, for the first time in the remembered history of this Republic, did its college and university students assert a responsibility for their own education, demand a part in the process? Are we really to believe with some of our politicians that the whole thing was the result of a mysterious, countrywide conspiracy among the hairier of the young directed perhaps by a sinister professor somewhere? Or is it open to us to consider that the crisis in the university may actually have been what we called it: a crisis *in* the university — a crisis in education itself precipitated by a revolution in ideas, a revolution in the ideas of a new generation of mankind?

There are those who believe we must find the answer to that question where we find the question: in the decade in which it was asked. Franklin Ford, then dean of the Faculty of Arts and

17

Sciences at Harvard and one of the ablest and most admired of university administrators, attributed this changed mentality in great part to "the particular malaise of the sixties." Undertaking to explain to his colleagues his view of what we have come to call "student unrest," Dean Ford defined it in terms of concentric circles, the most important of which would include students who had been profoundly hurt by the anguish of these recent years: "The thought-benumbing blows of successive assassinations, the equally tragic though more comprehensible crisis of the cities, the growing bitterness of the poor amid the self-congratulations of affluence, the even greater bitterness of black Americans, rich or poor . . . all these torments of our day have hit thoughtful young people with peculiar force . . . Youth is a time of extreme vulnerability to grief and frustration, as well as a time of impatient, generous sympathy." And to all this, Dean Ford continued, must be added the war in Vietnam, which he saw as poisoning and exacerbating everything else, contributing "what can only be described as [a sense] of horror."

Most of us — perhaps I should qualify that by saying most of those with whom I talk — would agree. We would agree, that is to say, that the war in Vietnam poisoned the American mind. We would agree that the affluent society — more precisely the affluent half-society — has turned out to be a sick society, for the affluent half as well as for the other. We would agree that the cancer of the cities, the animal hatred of the races, the bursting pustule of violence, has hurt us all and particularly those of us who are young and they in particular *because* they are young, because, being young, they are generous, they are vulnerable. We would agree to all this, and we would agree in consequence that there is a relationship between the malaise in the universities and Dean Ford's "particular malaise of the sixties."

But would we agree, reflecting on those considerations and this conclusion, that it is the tragic events of that decade which, alone, are the root cause — the effective cause — of the unrest of which Dean Ford was speaking? If the public bitterness, the brutality, the suffering of the last few years were the effective cause, would the *university* be the principal target of resentment? If Vietnam were the heart of the trouble, would the university curriculum be attacked — the methods of teaching, the teachers themselves? Would the reaction not have expressed itself, as it once did, at the Pentagon?

What was resented, clearly, was again not only the state of the Republic, the state of the world, but some relation or lack of relation between the state of the Republic, the state of the world, and the process of education — the process of education in the university.

But what relation or lack of relation? A direct, a one-to-one, relationship? Was the university blamed *because* the war was being fought, *because* the ghetto existed, *because* the affluent society was the vulgar, dull, unbeautiful society we saw in our more ostentatious cities? Was the demand of the young a demand that the university should alter its instruction and its practices so as to put an end to this ugliness, these evils — reshape this society?

There were some undergraduates, certainly, who took this position. There were some who wanted to bring the weight and influence of the university to bear directly on the solution of economic and social problems through the management of the university's real estate and endowments. There were others who wished to direct its instruction toward specific evils by establishing courses in African affairs and urban studies. Both attitudes were familiar: they were standard demands of student political organizations. They were also reasonable — reasonable at least in purpose if not always in form. But did they go to the heart of the matter? Was this direct relationship of specific instruction to specific need — of specific land-use program to specific land-use evil — the relation undergraduates had in mind when they complained, as they did over and over, that their courses were not "relevant," that their education did not "respond to their needs," or "preach to their condition"? Was it only "applicability," only immediate pertinence, that the generation of the young demanded of us? Was the deep, almost undefinable restlessness of the student generation — the dark unhappiness of which Senator Muskie spoke — an unhappiness which Centers of Urban Studies, however necessary, could cure?

I do not think so. The distress, the very real and generous suffering and distress of an entire generation of young men and young women, was related certainly to the miseries of the sixties, but it was not founded in them and it would not disappear when they vanished. The "relevance" these students spoke of was not relevance to the newspapers. It was relevance to their own lives, to the living of their lives, to themselves as men and women living. And their resentment, their very real resentment and distress, rose not only from the tragedies and mischances of the sixties but from a human situation, a total human situation, involving human life as human life, which had been three generations in the making.

At the time of the Sorbonne riots, a French politician spoke in terms of apocalypse: We had come to a time like the fall of

The Revolt of the Diminished Man

Rome when civilizations collapse because belief is dead. What was actually happening in Paris and elsewhere was, of course, the precise opposite. Belief, passionate belief, had come alive for the first time in the century and, with it, rage and violence. The long diminishment, the progressive diminution, of value put upon man, upon the idea of man, in modern society had met the revulsion of a generation of the young who condemned it in all its aspects, left as well as right, Communist as well as capitalist, the indifference of the Marxist bureaucracies as well as the bureaucratic indifference of the industrial West.

This diminishment of the idea of man has been a long time in the making. I will not claim for my generation that we witnessed its beginning, I will assert only that we were the first to record it where alone it could be recorded. The arts with us became aware of a flatness in human life, a loss of depth as though a dimension had somehow dropped from the world — as though our human shadows had deserted us. The great metaphor of the journey of mankind — Ulysses among the mysteries and monsters — reduced itself in our youth to that other Ulysses among the privies and the pubs of Dublin, Ireland. Cleopatra on her flowery barge floated through a Saturday night in the Bloomsbury twenties. Even death itself was lessened: the multitudes of Dante's damned crossed T. S. Eliot's London Bridge, commuters in the morning fog. Nothing was left remarkable beneath the visiting moon.

And in the next generation — the generation of Joyce's secretary and disciple, Samuel Beckett — the testimony of the arts went on. The banality turned to impotence and numbness and paralysis, a total anesthesia of the soul. Leopold Bloom no longer maundered through the musty Dublin streets. He was incapable even of maundering, incapable of motion. He sat to his neck in sand, like a head of rotting celery in an autumn garden, and waited, or did not even wait — just sat there. While as for Cleopatra — Cleopatra was an old man's youthful memory played back upon a worn-out tape.

The arts are honest witnesses in these matters. Pound was right enough, for all the well-known plethora of language, when he wrote in praise of Joyce's *Ulysses* that "it is a summary of pre-war Europe, the blackness and mess and muddle of a 'civilization,'" and that "Bloom very much *is* the mess." The arts, moreover, are honest witnesses in such matters not only when they achieve works of art as with Joyce and Eliot and frequently with Beckett. They testify even when they fail. The unpoem, the nonpainting of the sixties, the play that does not play, all bear their penny's worth of witness. The naked, half-embarrassed boy exhibiting his pudenda on an Off-Off-Broadway stage is not an actor, nor is his shivering gesture a dramatic act, but still he testifies. He is the last, sad, lost reincarnation of L. Bloom, the resurrection of the head of celery. Odysseus on his lonely raft in the god-infested sea has come to this.

What was imagined in Greece, reimagined in the Renaissance, carried to a passion of pride in Europe of the Enlightenment and to a passion of hope in the Republic of the New World — John Adams's hope as well as Jefferson's and Whitman's; Lincoln's which he called "the last, best hope" — all this grimaces in pitiful derision of itself in that nude, sad, shivering figure. And we see it or we hear about it and protest. But protest *what?* The nakedness! The morals of the playwright! Undoubtedly the playwright needs correction in his morals and above all in the practice of his art, but in his *vision?* His *perception?* Is he the first to see this? On the contrary, his most obvious failure as playwright is precisely the fact that he is merely one of thousands in a thronging, long contemporary line — a follower of fashion. He testifies as hundreds of his betters have been testifying now for years — for generations — near a century.

Why have they so testified? They cannot tell you. The artist's business is to see and to show, not answer why: to see as no one else can see, and to show as nothing else can show, but not to explain. He knows no more of explanation than another, And yet *we* cannot help but wonder why — why the belief in man has foundered; why it has foundered *now* — precisely *now* — now at the moment of our greatest intellectual triumphs, our never-equaled technological mastery, our electronic miracles. Why was man a wonder to the Greeks — to Sophocles of all the Greeks — when he could do little more than work a ship to windward, ride a horse, and plow the earth, while now that he knows the whole of modern science he is a wonder to no one — certainly not to Sophocles' successors and least of all, in any case, to himself?

There is no easy answer, though thoughtful men are beginning to suggest that an answer may be found and that, when it is, it may very well relate precisely to this vast new knowledge. George W. Morgan states the position in his *The Human Predicament:* "The sheer weight of accumulated but uncontrolled knowledge and information, of print, views, discoveries, and interpretations, of methods and techniques, inflicts a paralyzing sense of impotence. The mind is overwhelmed by a constant fear of its ignorance . . . The individual man, feeling unable to gain a valid perspective of the world and of himself, is forced to regard both as consisting of innumerable isolated parts to be relinquished, for knowledge and control, to a legion of experts." All this, says Mr. Morgan, diminishes human understanding in the very process of augmenting human knowledge. It also, I should wish to add, diminishes something else. It diminishes man. For man, as the whole of science as well as the whole of poetry will demonstrate, is not what he thinks he knows, but what he thinks he *can* know, can become.

But however much or little we comprehend of the cause of our paradoxical diminishment in our own eyes at the moment of our greatest technological triumphs, we cannot help but understand a little of its consequences and particularly its relation to the crisis in the university. Without the belief in man, the university is a contradiction in terms. The business of the university is education at its highest level, and the business of education at its highest level is the relation of men to their lives. But how is the university to concern itself with the relation of men to their lives, to the living of their lives, to the world in which their lives are lived, without the bold assumption, the brave, improbable hypothesis, that these lives matter, that these men count — that Odysseus on his battered, drifting raft still stands for a reality we take for real?

And how can a generation of the young, born into the world of the diminished man and in revolt against it — in revolt against its indifference to humanity in its cities and in its wars and in the weapons of its wars — how can a generation of the young help but demand some teaching from the universities which will interpret all this horror and make cause against it?

Centuries ago in a world of gods and mysteries and monsters when man's creativity, his immense creative powers, had been, as Berdyaev put it "paralyzed by the Middle Ages" — when men had been diminished in their own eyes by the demeaning dogma of the Fall — centuries ago the university conceived an intellectual and spiritual position which released mankind into a new beginning, a rebirth, a Renaissance. What is demanded of us now in a new age of gods and mysteries and monsters — not without dogmas and superstitions of its own — is a second humanism that will free us from our new paralysis of soul, as the earlier humanism freed us from that other. If it was human significance which was destroyed by the Middle Ages, it is human significance which we ourselves are now again destroying. We are witnessing, as the British critic F. R. Leavis phrases it, the elimination of that "day-by-day creativity of human response which manifests itself in the significances and values without which there is no reality — nothing but emptiness that has to be filled with drink, sex, eating, background music, and . . . the papers and the telly."

Mr. Leavis, not the most optimistic of dons on any occasion, believes that something might be done to revive "the creative human response that maintains cultural continuity" and that gives human life a meaning. I, with fewer qualifications to speak, would go much further. I would say that a conscious and determined effort to conceive a new humanism, which would do for our darkness what that earlier humanism did for the darkness of the Middle Ages, is not only a present dream but a present possibility, and that it is a present possibility not despite the generation of the sixties — but because of it.

That generation was not perhaps as sophisticated politically as it — or its activist spokesmen — would have had us think. Its moral superiority to earlier generations may not have been in every instance as great as it believed. But one virtue it did possess to a degree not equaled by any generation in this century: It believed in man.

It was an angry generation, yes, but its resentment was not the disgust of the generation for which Beckett spoke. Its resentment was not a resentment of our human life but a resentment *on behalf* of human life; not an indignation that we exist on the earth but that we *permit* ourselves to exist in a selfishness and and wretchedness and squalor which we have the means to abolish. Resentment of this kind is founded, can only be founded, on belief in man. And belief in man — a return to the belief in man — is the reality on which a new age can be built.

Thus far, that new belief has been used by the young largely as a weapon — as a justification of an indictment of earlier generations for their exploitation and debasement of human life and earth. When it is allowed to become itself — when the belief in man becomes an affirmative effort to re-create the life of man — the crisis in the university may well become the triumph of the university.

For it is only the university in this technological age which can save us from ourselves. And the university, as we now know, can only function effectively when it functions as a common labor of all its generations dedicated to the highest purpose of them all.

3
Master or Man

❧

W HETHER WE think much about it or not, most of us are aware that the American mood, perhaps even the American character, has changed. There are few manifestations any longer of the old American self-assurance which so irritated Dickens when he traveled among us in the last century. Instead, there is a sense of frustration so perceptible that even our politicians, or some of them, have attempted to exploit it. One of the smartest of them invented what he called the Silent Majority — a collection of Americans so dispirited that they had ceased to speak even though they still had most of the votes — while another used the prevalent mood to create a military issue which he could ride to power: the country was frustrated, he said, because a primitive "water-buffalo economy" had refused to surrender at the sight of our military superiority, and the thing to do was to bomb it off the map. The first got himself elected president as leader of the Silent Majority but turned out to have nothing to say to the general frustration except to aggravate it, while the other might have won his party's nomination for the presidency had he not had the bad luck to run against an unusually cheerful man who retained the fundamental elements of common sense.

The great American frustration, it turned out, was something a good deal saner and quite a bit more serious than either Mr. Nixon or Mr. Reagan guessed, and what it involved was neither party politics nor military strategy in Vietnam. It was — and is — something deeper and more troubling: a numb, unformed, persistent sense like the hinting pinch of a pain which is not yet mortal, that we have somehow lost control of our destiny. And not our military destiny only, or our political destiny, but our human destiny as men. It is a sense we have had in one form or another for a long time now, but not as an explicit, a formulated fear until we found ourselves deep in the present century with its faceless slaughters, its mindless violence, its fabulous triumphs over space and time and matter ending in terrors space and time and matter never held. Before that there were only hints and intimations, but they were felt, they were recorded where all the hints and intimations are recorded — in poems, fictions, works of art. From the beginning of what we used to call the industrial revolution — what we see today more clearly as a sort of technological coup d'état — men and women, particularly men and women of imaginative sensibility, have seen that something was happening to the human role in the shaping of civilization.

A curious automatism, human in origin but not human in action, seemed to be taking over. Cities were being built and rebuilt not with human purposes in mind but with technological means at hand. It was no longer the neighborhood which fixed the shape and limits of the town but the communications system, the power grid. Technology, our grandfathers said, "advanced" and it was literally true: it was technology which was beating the tambours, leading the march. Buildings crowded into the air not because their occupants had any particular desire to lift them there, but because the invention of electric elevators and new methods of steel and glass construction made these ziggurats possible and the possibility presented itself as economic compulsion.

Wildness and silence disappeared from the countryside, sweetness fell from the air, not because anyone wished them to vanish or fall but because throughways had to floor the meadows with cement to carry the automobiles which advancing technology produced first by the thousands and then by the thousand thousands. Tropical beaches turned into high-priced slums where thousand-room hotels elbowed each other for glimpses of once-famous surf not because those who loved the beaches wanted them there but because enormous jets could bring a million tourists every year — and therefore did.

The result, seen in a glimpse here, a perception there, was a gradual change in our attitude toward ourselves as men, toward the part we play as men in the direction of our lives. It was a confused change. We were proud — in England, and even more in America, raucously proud — of our technological achievements, but we were aware also, even from the beginning, that these achievements were not altogether ours or, more precisely, not altogether ours to direct, to control — that the *process* had somehow taken over leaving the purpose to shift for itself so that we, the ostensible managers of the process, were merely its beneficiaries.

Not, of course, that we complained of that, at least in the beginning. A hundred years ago, with the rare exception of a

Dickens or a Zola, we were amenable enough — amenable as children at a Christmas party. Inventions showered on our heads; steam engines and electric lights and telegraph messages and all the rest. We were up to our knees, up to our necks, in Progress. And technology had made it all possible. Science was the giver of every good and perfect gift. If there were aspects of the new world which were not perfect — child labor for example — progress would take care of them. If the ugliness and filth and smoke of industrial cities offended us, we put up with them for the sake of the gaslights and the central heating. We were rich and growing richer.

Nevertheless the uneasiness remained and became more and more evident in our books, our paintings, our music — even the new directions of our medical sciences. Who were *we* in this strange new world? What part did *we* play in it? Someone had written a new equation somewhere, pushed the doors of ignorance back a little, entered the darkened room of knowledge by one more step. Someone else had found a way to make use of that new knowledge, put it to work. Our lives had changed but without *our* changing them, without our intending them to change. Improvements had appeared, and we had accepted them. We had bought Mr. Ford's machines by the hundreds of thousands. We had ordered radios by the millions and then installed television sets. And now we took to the air. Flew from city to city, from continent to continent, from climate to climate, following summer up and down the earth like birds. We were new men in a new life in a new world . . . but a world *we* had not made — had not, at least, intended to make.

And a new world, moreover, that we were increasingly un-sure, as time went by, we would have wanted to make. We wanted its conveniences, yes. Its comforts, certainly. But the world as a world to live in? As a human world? It was already obvious by the beginning of this century that many of our artists and writers — those not so silent observers of the human world who sit in its windows and lurk in its doorways watching — were not precisely in love with the modern world; were, indeed, so little in love with it that they had turned against life itself, accepting absurdity and terror in its place and making of human hopelessness the only human hope. And there were other nearer, stranger witnesses. Before the century was two-thirds over, numbers of our children — extraordinary numbers if you stop to think about it — were to reject, singly and secretly, or publicly in curious refugee encampments, the whole community of our modern lives, and most particularly those aspects of our lives which were most modern: their conveniences, their comforts . . . their affluence.

It was inevitable under these circumstances that some sort of confrontation should occur between the old idea of man as the liver of his own life, the shaper of his own existence, and the new idea of world, the newly autonomous world — world autonomous in its economic laws, as the Marxists hoped, or autonomous in its scientific surge, its technological compulsions, as some in the West began to fear. And, of course, the confrontation did occur: first in rather fatuous academic ructions in which science and the humanities were made to quarrel with each other in the universities, and then, in 1945, at Hiroshima. What happened at Hiroshima was not only that a scientific breakthrough — "breakthrough" in the almost literal sense — had occurred and that a great part of the population of a city had been burned to death, but that the problem of the relation of the triumphs of modern science to the human purposes of man had been explicitly defined, and the whole question of the role of humanity in the modern scientific age had been exposed in terms not even the most unthinking could evade.

Prior to Hiroshima, it had still been possible — increasingly difficult but still possible — to believe that science was by nature a human tool obedient to human wishes and that the world science and its technology could create would therefore be a human world, reflecting our human needs, our human purposes. After Hiroshima it was obvious that the loyalty of science was not to humanity but to truth — its own truth — and that the law of science was not the law of the good — what humanity thinks of as good, meaning moral, decent, humane — but the law of the possible. What it is *possible* for science to know science must know. What it is *possible* for technology to do technology will have done. If it is possible to split the atom, then the atom must be split. Regardless. Regardless of . . . anything.

There was a time, just after Hiroshima, when we tried — we in the United States, at least — to escape from that haunting problem by blaming the scientists as individuals: the scientists, in particular, who had made the bomb — the mysterious workers in the cellars at Stagg Field and the laboratories of the Manhattan Project. And the scientists themselves, curious as it now may seem, cooperated; many of them, many of the best, assuming, or attempting to assume, burdens of personal guilt or struggling, somehow, anyhow, to undo what had been done.

I remember more vividly perhaps than anything else which happened to me in those years — a late winter evening after Hiroshima in a study at the Institute at Princeton — Einstein's study, I think — where Niels Bohr, who was as great a man as he was a physicist, walked up and down for hours beside the rattling radiators urging me to go to President Truman, whom I barely knew, to remind him that there had been an understanding between Mr. Roosevelt and the scientists about the future neutralization of the bomb. I guessed that Bohr, even as he talked that evening, realized there was nothing Mr. Truman or anyone on earth could do to unknow what was known. And yet he walked up and down the freezing study talking. Things of course, *were* "done" — attempted anyway. In the brief time when we alone possessed what was called "the secret," the American government offered to share it with the world (the Baruch Plan) for peaceful exploitation. What we proposed, though we did not put it in these words, was that humanity as a whole should assert its control of science, or at least of this particular branch of science — nuclear physics — limiting its pursuit of possibility to possibilities which served mankind. But the Russians with their dogma of the dialectics of matter, demurred. They preferred to put their trust in *things*, and within a few short months their trust was justified: they had the bomb themselves.

The immediate effect in the United States was, of course, the mounting fear of Russia which fed the Cold War abroad and made the black plague of McCarthyism possible at home. But there was also a deeper and more enduring consequence. Our original American belief in our human capability, our human capacity to manage our affairs ourselves, "govern ourselves," faltered with our failure to control the greatest and most immediate of human dangers. We began to see science as a kind of absolute beyond our reach, beyond our understanding even;

known, if it was known at all, through proxies who, like priests in other centuries, could not tell us what they knew.

In short, our belief in ourselves declined at the very moment when the Russian belief in the mechanics of the universe confirmed itself. No one talked any longer of a Baruch Plan, or even remembered that there had been one. The freedom of science to follow the laws of absolute possibility to whatever conclusions had been established, or so we thought, as the unchallengeable fixed assumption of our age, and the freedom of technology to invent whatever world it happened to invent was taken as the underlying law of modern life. It was enough for a manufacturer of automobiles to announce on television that he had a better idea — any better idea: pop-open gas-tank covers or headlights that hide by day. No one thought any longer of asking whether his new idea matched a human purpose.

What was happening in those years, as the bitterly satirical fictions of the period never tired of pointing out, was that we were ceasing to think of ourselves as men, as self-governing men, as proudly self-governing makers of a new nation, and were becoming instead a society of consumers: recipients — grateful recipients — of the blessings of a technological civilization. We no longer talked in the old way of the American Proposition, either at home or abroad — particularly abroad. We talked instead of the American Way of Life. It never crossed our minds apparently — or if it did we turned our minds away — that a population of consumers, though it may constitute an affluent society, can never compose a nation in the great, the human, sense.

But the satirical novels, revealing as they were, missed the essential fact that we were becoming a population of consumers not because we preferred to think of ourselves in this somewhat less than noble role but because we were no longer able to think of ourselves in that other role — the role our grandfathers had conceived for us two hundred years ago. We were not, and knew we were not, Whitman's *Pioneers! O Pioneers!* We did not even know that famous line of his which reads: "Solitary, singing in the West, I strike up for a new world."

It is here, rather than in the floundering failures and futile disappointments of Vietnam, that this famous frustration of ours is rooted. Vietnam alone, disastrous as that whole experience was, could never have produced, in a confident and self-reliant people such as the Americans once were, a mood like the American mood. Not even the riots of the sixties could have afflicted us, as they did, if we had believed that our principal business was the making of a nation, the government of ourselves. Indeed the riots were, if anything, the consequence, not the cause, of our self-doubt — or, more precisely, the consequence of the *actual* causes of that doubt. It is not without significance that the targets of the mobs in the burning streets were supermarkets and television outlets rather than the courthouses and city halls which would have drawn the mobs of earlier times. Courthouses and city halls stand — or stood once — for the American Proposition. Supermarkets and television outlets are the symbols of the American Way of Life. Mobs strike for the Bastille in any rising and the Bastille in the United States today is whatever stands for the American Way of Life: the goods and services, the material wealth, which the majority claim as the mark of their Americanism and which the minority are denied.

It was because we were unwilling to recognize this fact and unable to face the crisis as a crisis in the long struggle for the creation of a true Republic — because, indeed, we were no longer primarily concerned with the creation of a true Republic — that the majority responded to these riots with nothing but a demand for more police and more repression, while the Congress sat impotent and paralyzed in Washington.

Which means of course, however we put it, that we no longer believed in man. And it is that fact which raises, in its turn, the most disturbing of all the swarming questions which surround us: How did we come to this defeated helplessness? How were we persuaded of our impotence as men? What convinced us that the fundamental law of a scientific age must be the scientific law of possibility — what can be must be — and that our human part must be a passive part, a subservient part, the part of the recipient, the beneficiary . . . the victim?

Have the scientists taught us this? A year or so ago, one of the greatest of living scientists told an international gathering composed of other scientists: "We must not ask where science and technology are taking us, but rather how we can manage science and technology so that they can help us get where we want to go." It is not reported that Dr. René Dubos was shouted down by his audience, and yet what he was asserting was precisely what we as a people seem to have dismissed as unthinkable: that "we," which apparently means mankind, must abandon our modern practice of asking where science and technology are "taking *us*," and must ask instead how *we* can "manage" science and technology, so that they will help us to achieve *our* purposes as men.

Dr. Dubos, it appears, scientist though he is and great scientist, believes rather more in man than we do. Why, then, do we believe so little? Perhaps we can answer that question best by asking another: How was our original, American belief in man achieved? Where did it come from? Thomas Jefferson who had as much to do with the definition of our American belief as anyone, reflected on that subject toward his life's end. It was that famous trio at William and Mary, he decided, who "fixed" his "destinies." It was his education in his college, the teaching of Small and Wythe and the rest, which shaped his mind, gave it its direction. John Adams would have said the same and doubtless did: it was in Harvard College that he found those Greeks and Romans who taught him what a man could be and therefore *should*.

Is it *our* education, then, which has shaped the very different estimate of man we live by? In part, I think; in considerable part. Education, particularly higher education, has altered its relation to the idea of man in fundamental ways since Adams's day and Jefferson's. From the time when Harvard President Charles Eliot introduced the elective system there — from the time, that is to say, of the renunciation by the university of an intention to produce a certain *kind* of man, a man shaped by certain models, certain texts — the university's concern with "man" as such has grown less and less and its concern with what it calls "subjects" has become greater and greater. The important thing has become the academic "offering" (revealing word): the range of subjects from which the student, with his eye on his career, may choose. And the ultimate consequence, only too evident in the time we live in, has been the vocationalization of the high schools. The college no longer exists to produce men *qua* men, men prepared for life in a society of men, but to produce men as specialized experts, men prepared for employment in an industry or a profession.

"Getting ahead in the world," says Allen Tate, "is now the purpose of education and the University must therefore provide education for our time, not for all time: it must discover and then give to society what society thinks it wants . . ." Some of us, looking at the present state of American society — the decay of its cities, the bewilderment of its citizens — may wonder whether the university has really provided "education for our time," but no one, I think, will deny that Allen Tate's emphatic irony has its bite. The vocationalism which a technological society demands of the graduate schools has produced a secondary vocationalism which the graduate schools impose on the colleges, and the result is that undergraduate education — far more important to the preparation for manhood than graduate education — is increasingly tarnished by the vocational taint.

What is happening, and in the greatest universities as well as in the less great, is that the entire educational process is becoming fixed — hung-up, as the phrase goes now — on its vocational end result. The job out there in the profession or the industry dictates the "training" (their word, not mine) in the graduate schools, and the graduate schools dictate the preparation in the colleges, and the whole system congeals from the top down like a pond freezing. The danger is that the society may congeal with it, for nothing is more certain in the history of our kind than the fact that frozen societies perish.

As specialized, professional training, higher education in the United States today is often magnificent. Young doctors are better and better "trained" as their specialties become more specialized: so much better that it is now a recommendation in almost any field to say of a young doctor that he is young. Student physicists in the great graduate schools are so notoriously productive at twenty-two that a professional physicist of thirty regards himself, or is regarded by his juniors, as middle-aged. But the educated *man*, the man capable, not of providing specialized answers but of asking the great and liberating questions by which humanity makes its way through time, is not more frequently encountered than he was two hundred years ago. On the contrary, he is rarely discovered in public life at all.

I am not arguing — though I deeply believe — that the future of the Republic and the hope for a recovery of its old vitality and confidence depend on the university. I am confining myself to Dr. Dubos's admonition that we must give up the childishness of our present attitude toward science and technology — our constant question where *they* are taking *us* — and begin instead to ask how *we* can manage *them* "so that they can help us get where we want to go." "Where we want to go" depends, of course, on ourselves. If our conception of ourselves as the university teaches it or fails to teach it is the conception of the applicant preparing for his job, the professional preparing for his profession, then the question will not be answered because it will not be asked. But if our conception of ourselves as the university teaches it is that of men preparing to be men, to achieve themselves as men, then the question will be asked *and* answered because it cannot be avoided. Where do we want to go? Where men can be most themselves. How should science and technology be managed? To help us become what we can be.

There is no quarrel between the humanities and the sciences. There is only a need, common to them both, to put the idea of man back where it once stood, at the focus of our lives; to make the end of education the preparation of men to be men, and so to restore to mankind — and above all to this nation of mankind — a conception of humanity with which humanity can live.

The frustration — and it is a real and debasing frustration — will not leave us until we believe in ourselves again, assume again the mastery of our lives, the management of our means.

4

The Premise at the Center

W HAT IS a collection of books? Which can be reversed to read: what is a book in a collection? — a book to a library? — to a librarian? Is it merely the unit of collection, a more or less fungible (as the lawyers put it) object made of paper, print, and protective covering that fulfills its bibliographical destiny by being classified as to subject and catalogued by author and title and properly shelved? Or is it something very different? Is it still a book? Is it, indeed, something more now than a book, being a book selected to compose with other books a library? But, if so, what has it become?

When he was seventy-four years old the Cretan novelist Nikos Kazantzakis began a book. He called it *Report to Greco*, Greco being, of course, the older and even more famous Cretan who painted the *Burial of Count Orgaz* and other canvases. *Report* is the operative word in this title: Kazantzakis thought of himself as a soldier reporting to his commanding officer on a mortal mission — his life. "I collect my tools: sight, smell, touch, taste, hearing, intellect . . . I call upon my memory to remember, I assemble my life from the air, place myself soldier-like before the general and make my report . . . For Greco is kneaded from the same Cretan soil as I and is able to understand me better than all the strivers of past and present. Did he not leave the same red track upon the stones?"

Well, there is only one *Report to Greco*, but no true book — no book truly part of a true library — was ever anything else than a report. Shakespeare used a different — and, being Shakespeare, a better — metaphor but it comes to the same thing. Lear speaks it to Cordelia at that sunshine moment toward the play's end before the deluge of the dark. They will go off, says Lear, the two of them, to their prison cell and "take upon's the mystery of things / As though we were God's spies." All poems worthy to be preserved as poems are written so — by God's spies beneath the burden of the mystery — and so are all other gathered writings of whatever kind however we may classify them, whether as fictions or as science, as history or philosophy or whatever. A true book is a report upon the mystery of existence; it tells what has been seen in a man's life in the world — touched there, thought of, tasted.

But it does more, too, as Kazantzakis' *Report* does more: it interprets the signs, brings word back from the frontiers, from the distances. Whether it offers its news in a live voice or is left, like Emily Dickinson's snippets of paper tied up with loops of thread, to be found by an astonished sister afterward in a little drawer, it speaks of the world, of our life in the world. Everything we have in the books on which our libraries are founded — Euclid's figures, Leonardo's notes, Newton's explanations, Cervantes' myth, Sappho's broken songs, even the vast surge of Homer — everything is a report of one kind or another and the sum of all of them together is our little knowledge of our world and of ourselves. Call a book *Das Kapital* or *The Voyage of the Beagle* or *Theory of Relativity* or *Alice in Wonderland* or *Moby Dick*, it is still what Kazantzakis called his book — what Shakespeare intended by that immortal metaphor — it is still a "report" — upon the "mystery of things."

But if this is what a book is in a library, then a library, considered not as a collection of objects that happen to be books but as a number of books that have been chosen to constitute a library, is an extraordinary thing. It is not at all what it is commonly supposed to be even by men who describe themselves as intellectuals — perhaps I should say particularly by men who describe themselves as intellectuals. It is not a sort of scholarly filling station where students of all ages can repair to get themselves supplied with a tankful of titles; not an academic facility to be judged by the quantity of its resources and the promptness of its services. On the contrary it is an achievement in and of itself — one of the greatest of human achievements because it combines and justifies so many others. That its card catalogues and bibliographical machinery are useful no one doubts: modern scholarship would be impossible without them. That its housing and safekeeping arrangements are vital, essential, necessary, goes without saying. But what is more important in a library than anything else — than everything else — is the fact that it exists.

For the existence of a library, the fact of its existence, is, in itself and of itself, an assertion — a proposition nailed like Luther's to the door of time. By standing where it does at the center of the university — which is to say at the center of our intellectual lives — with its books in a certain order on its shelves and its cards in a certain structure in their cases, the true library asserts that there is indeed a "mystery of things." Or, more precisely, it asserts that the reason why the "things" compose a mystery is that they seem to mean: that they fall, when gathered together, into a kind of relationship, a kind of wholeness, as though all these different and dissimilar reports, these bits and pieces of experience, manuscripts in bottles, messages from long before, from deep within, from miles away, *belonged* together and might, if understood together, spell out the meaning which the mystery implies.

For the point is that without the implication of meaning, which is to say the premise of meaning, there can be no mystery anywhere. The dark is not mysterious: it is merely dark. Even the greatest of physicists, even Einstein himself, when he wished to speak of the universe as science observes it, spoke of it as standing before us "like a great, eternal riddle." And a riddle, needless to say, even a scientist's riddle, even a scientist's eternal riddle, even a scientist's eternal riddle of the dimensions of the universe, is something which, by hypothesis, exists to be solved.

It is this fact — the fact of the library's implicit assertion of the possibility of meaning — which provides the drama of the university in the world we live in. Whatever a library may have been back in the days of Mr. Carnegie's kindness when all good Scots believed that reading resulted in understanding and the rest of the world believed the Scots — whatever a library may have been in those days, there is a taste of irony about it now and more than a stir of drama. Our world — at least that part of our world which we call the West — no longer hopes for meanings. Even the philosophers, whose goal was once what they called A Final Explanation, concern themselves these days with something less — with a process. And as for the intellectuals, more numerous as confidence in the intellect declines, their shuttling caravan has almost come to rest at the last oasis on the road to Prester John — the sandy spring of the Absurd. Their leaders may desert them. Ionesco himself, author of *The Bald Soprano*, may regret the disappearance of meaning from the world. But the caravan holds firm beneath the dying date trees. "There was a time, long, long ago," says Ionesco, "when the world seemed to man to be so charged with meaning that he didn't have time to ask himself questions . . . The whole world was like a theater in which the elements, the forests, the oceans, the rivers, the mountains and the plains, the bushes and each plant played an incomprehensible role that man tried to understand, tried to explain to himself . . . Exactly when," says Ionesco, "was the world emptied of substance, exactly when were the signs no longer signs?" To which the caravan responds with a single voice that there was a time long, long ago when Ionesco's answer to all those draughty questions would have been "Who cares?" Certainly the caravan doesn't care. Meanings went out for it with Hiroshima. All that's left us is absurdity. Unless you count despair.

But if Ionesco's complaint is out of fashion, what shall we say of the Great Affirmation spelled out in almost visible letters above the door of any library? Those Reports to Greco on its shelves exist in a relationship which implies that the library's business is relationship. But the generation the library is to serve has been raised in the belief that what matters is not the relationships which compose our lives but something very different — something called relevance — the relevance of each aspect of existence to ourselves. Not the weft and weave that surrounds us, the mystery of things, the riddle of the universe, the implicitness of meaning, but an immediate identification of each thing with each self on the assumption that there is no meaning and that only self is real. Love, for example, which is all relationship, total relationship, infinite connection, is made relevant by turning it to sex which is connection and nothing more. Death, which was once, in the old world of relationship, the perspective of everything, the distance that turns the mountains blue, becomes relevant by becoming conclusion: not even an exit — just an end.

And life itself, once that infinite possibility, that prison cell where the defeated king could take upon himself and his mild daughter the vastness of our human wonder, is made a prison cell and nothing more — the ultimate relevance — in a solitary and absurd confinement where nothing, not even Godot, ever comes and nothing answers but the idiot whimper of self-pity.

Oh, there is drama enough in a library, irony enough, but which way truly does the irony cut? Is it the library's implicit assertion of the immanence of meaning that has become ridiculous in our fuddled time, or is it the tired caravan of intellectual fashion stumbling toward the Mountains of the Moon? I do not know the answer but I know something that can say it. I know that meaninglessness is just as much a matter of belief as meaning. The caravan of the intellectuals would have you think that someone has *discovered* meaninglessness out there beyond us in the desert — in the infinities of space — and brought it home like a phoenix egg to prove the world is void. Nothing could be more childish. Meaninglessness, like meaning, is a conclusion in the mind, a reading, an interpretation.

And science — honest science — knows it. Jacques Monod, the French biochemist who saw living beings as chemical ma-

45

chines that construct themselves out of chemical chance, concluded that the process of life is blind and man an accident. But he reached this conclusion, as he himself acknowledged, by way of his belief in theories of quantum mechanics in which other scientists, Einstein among the lot, are unable to believe. "A mutation," wrote M. Monod, "is in itself a microscopic event, a quantum event, to which the principle of uncertainty consequently applies." But to Einstein the consequence did not apply because the assumption was unsound. Einstein, as Gerald Holton puts it, was a scientist "fighting for a causal physics" who assumed "a rational God of causal laws who would not play dice with the universe." Whether Einstein's assumption is right or M. Monod's, is not, perhaps, for us, and certainly not for me, to say, but one thing is clear even to a scientific illiterate like myself: the issue between M. Monod and Einstein, or between their positions, is an issue of belief. Einstein made that clear enough. Quantum physics was to him a "false religion." And he said so. In so many words.

It would be helpful to us, with such a question to answer, if there were an Einstein of the world of letters to match that explicit Einstein in the world of science. For it is in the world of letters that the contemporary cult of meaninglessness has presented itself most flagrantly as something more than a cult, more than an opinion: as an established fact to be accepted with despair. And it is in the world of letters that this masquerade can do most damage. Critics may pursue the meaningless relentlessly, as they may pursue anything else that moves, without damage to their reputations or themselves. And playwrights, ambiguous reporters, may make their fortunes by it — they have. But the poor devil of a poet lives by meanings if he lives at all. Relationship is all he has to work with: that *analogie universelle* which Baudelaire discovered in the poems of two thousand years and which the poems not yet written still must seek. For the poet, the novelist — the artist in letters — to assert the meaninglessness of the world is the ultimate act of human folly, the act that ridicules itself. Even if the "principle of uncertainty" were established to the satisfaction of all science and M. Monod were right in his finding that no "master plan" exists for the construction of his "chemical machines," man would still exist. And it is precisely man who, through his arts, through his thought, through his Reports to Greco, has constructed meanings over millennia of time. Whether the universe has confirmed them or not. Job's demand for justice was shouted down by the voice from the whirlwind but Job, because he was a man, took back his life and lived it notwithstanding.

No, it is not the library, I think, that has become ridiculous by standing there against the dark with its books in order on its shelves. On the contrary the library, almost alone of the great monuments of civilization, stands taller now than it ever did before. The city — the American city at least — decays. The nation loses its grandeur, becomes what we call a "power," a Pentagon, a store of missiles. The university is no longer always certain what it is. But the library remains: a silent and enduring affirmation that the great Reports still speak, and not alone but somehow all together — that, whatever else is chance and accident, the human mind, that mystery, still seems to mean.

5

News from the Horse and Wagon

DOWN TO TEN OR FIFTEEN years ago the great American attic was the most popular institution in the country. There wasn't anyone from the fourth grade to the National Institute of Arts and Letters who wasn't concerned with those marble busts and crooked muskets and models of the Flying Cloud and portraits of Mr. Lincoln and all the rest. Millions were spent on restoring Colonial Williamsburg and putting the battlefields in order, marking the birthplaces, visiting Mr. Longfellow's house on Brattle Street, painting Mount Vernon.

And then, all at once, in the nineteen sixties, something went wrong. No one mentioned the attic any longer — not even the government in Washington. A Republican Attorney General, ordering the FBI to listen in on our telephone conversations, had nothing to say about that old book in the cowhide covers up on the attic shelf. And when college undergraduates looked around for junk to burn on their barricades, they raided the attic first without even knowing where they were or what those wooden eagles signified, those jackboots, those quotations in Latin.

What had happened, we were told, was all due to the smoke in the kitchen. No one thought about the attic anymore because the Asian war on the back of the stove gave off a stench you couldn't see through, let alone breathe, and the economy wouldn't come to a boil no matter how you turned the gas up, and as for the stuff in the big blue bowl on the kitchen table, you couldn't stir it with a bayonet: The mix had curdled. All of which was true, but not the whole truth. Something else had also happened to the attic. We had moved out as a nation. Beginning after the Second War we had left the old farm in the Shenandoah or up in the Berkshire Hills or down the Ohio and hired ourselves a flat or a back room in Philadelphia or Harlem or Detroit. We had become the first nation on earth to move bodily into Metropolis. And in Metropolis there is no attic. No place for an attic and therefore nothing to put in an attic. A farmhouse over the Deerfield River remembers. A Los Angeles flat can barely think back to breakfast.

Jefferson, of course, had foreseen all that. He knew that a free people needs space to be free in, time to move round in, room to store its past and thus prepare its future. By his life's end he had come to see that his old dream of a rural America was an illusion and that other means would have to be found — political means — educational means — to protect self-government. But not even Jefferson, unquestionably the farthest-seeing man of his century, foresaw the America of our day, a vast nation attempting to govern itself, not from farms and villages and towns but from enormous cities increasingly incapable of government of any kind.

Great underlying changes of that kind are never news — not the kind of thing that gets to be news — but nevertheless there have been journalistic signals, barometric readings, forecasts. James Reston and Tom Wicker of the *New York Times* have developed a kind of journalism which takes account, not only of the gossip at the long table in the Metropolitan Club, but of what our forefathers would have called talk of the Union, and every now and again one of their columns picks up reverberations that go deep as earthquake tremors.

One such was a column Tom Wicker wrote from Nantucket a few years back. Thanksgiving had been a magnificent day — northwest wind, bright sun, long streaks of foam on the wind-crisped water. Wicker had climbed those little hills behind Dionis Beach which face Great Point off across the shoals (could that be Great Point light?) and all at once the feel of the island came over him — the feel of that peculiar distance, part time and part the sea, which isolates you on an island anywhere and, more than most, on Nantucket. The moors had the heather color they take on in autumn and the gulls, I suppose, were glinting and vanishing off to seaward like the topsails of those long expected ships that never come. Nowhere on Nantucket are you very far from Quaker graves, sea-captains' graves — Macys, Starbucks, Coffins — and you get to looking toward the sea for sails.

So Tom Wicker was there in the bright wind thinking of wooden ships and year-long voyages and the young Republic of those days establishing herself upon the sea, and he was happy: refreshed, renewed, and happy. How far away, he thought, the world is! And it was then he understood what he was really thinking. He was choosing between past and present: between that innocent past of moors and sea before him and the menacing, shadowy present off behind to the south and west where the Hudson meets the sea — the modern, metropolitan present. That world which seemed so far away was, he suddenly understood, the real world . . . the reality. And with that understanding the same thing happened to Tom Wicker that happened to John Keats with the repetition of the word "forlorn" in the *Ode to a Nightingale:*

. . . *forlorn.*

Forlorn! The very word is like a bell
To toll me back from thee to my sole self . . .

Nantucket vanished. The sea which had delighted him with its streaks of vivid foam became a fraud — "deceitful" he told himself — "siren lures" — and before his column ended he had condemned himself and every other holiday visitor to the island for running away from life. "Those who long to return to nature and the ways of a quieter past," he wrote, "really are trying to escape the human race."

As a philosophical proposition that statement is not persuasive. Those same words or something very like them might have been spoken by the more respectable burghers of Concord, Massachusetts, when Henry Thoreau built his shack by Walden Pond, and yet the children and grandchildren of those who railed at Thoreau for rejecting humankind now read his account of that adventure to discover what a human being is. But philosophical soundness is not the point. Wicker is a reporter not an essayist — a reporter moreover who has the courage to put himself at the center of his scene as a way of dramatizing a situation — and, read as reportage, the Thanksgiving-Day journey to

Nantucket is a revealing, even a frightening story. For what it says is that the American past and the American present have come apart: not only that you can't go back anymore but that you *mustn't* go back anymore — that you are guilty if you go back — a runaway from reality.

Which means, in specific terms, that Metropolis and Republic have lost each other: that Metropolis is real and Republic a memory, an escapist dream. This I say is frightening. I mean that it is frightening if true. A nation no more than a man can exist without perpetual rebeginnings, a recurrent return to a recurrently recreative past. Only the psychologically sick attempt to live each day as a new beginning, meeting themselves for the first time in the mirror of every morning and dying with every dark. And as for Metropolis, which is psychologically sick if a human society ever was, to cut Los Angeles off from the Republic, to cut New York off, even Washington — most of all Washington — is to condemn these cities to disaster. If it is true that Metropolis is real and the high American past a delusion — true, I mean, that we *think* Metropolis is real — then it is also true that Nantucket will disappear as it disappears in Wicker's parable . . . taking the country with it.

But is it true? Is the parable true? It is true enough that we think Metropolis is real. We do believe — have come increasingly to believe over the past ten years — that the American Past is a kind of fairy tale, a delusion the government can pretend — but only pretend — to honor, a kind of Paul Revere fable the young should laugh at. After all, Metropolis *happened* didn't it? What could be more real than Harlem? Than Watts? And as for the American Past, what was it? Words largely — the Declaration of Independence — Mr. Lincoln. Words and wars — and everyone knows what wars are.

News from the Horse and Wagon

But it is there — precisely there — that the parable ought to go on and doesn't. Granted the truth of the observation — granted that we think of ourselves as more realistic than our naive and believing ancestors — granted that we see the American Proposition as an eighteenth-century error repealed by Karl Marx or whomever — does it follow that we are *right* to think what we think, see what we believe we see? Are we right, specifically, to believe that because Metropolis indubitably exists it *had* to exist? That we had no choice but to accept its existence? — still have no choice but to accept?

It is here that Americans like the Amish have something to say about the country *on* but not *in* which they live. The usual view of the Amish is that they are an anachronism, a people who got stuck in history back with the horse and wagon and an Old Testament God and other chronological oddities such as the arts of husbandry and domestic skills long unused and harmonious lives. We regard them as quaint — charming even — but as curiosities rather than contemporaries. A recent General Motors' advertisement says it all. General Motors, or its advertising agency, was apparently persuaded that the reason folks don't go touring as they used to is simply that there's nowhere left to tour. The cities won't serve — obviously. You can't see them for the smog or walk in them for the muggers. And as for the national scenery, scenery has a disconcerting way of turning into strip mines as you come around a curve in Kentucky or into virgin sewers as you follow a mountain trout stream in California. Which leaves you with nothing to head for but expressways connecting with other expressways. And you can't sell automobiles to go riding just for the ride unless you are willing to limit yourself to customers under seventeen.

So what General Motors, or its advertising agency, needed

53

was a place to go to and some unsung genius came up with the Amish country. It made a beautiful photograph. There you were in your brand new Chevrolet tooling along a country lane with a horse-drawn Amish wagon framed in your windshield. What better reason for driving a thousand miles? Better for *you*, that is, or for General Motors: the Amish farmer cramping into the ditch to let you go by, and the Chevrolet after you, and the Chevrolet after that, might have a somewhat different opinion. There is no particular satisfaction in being gawked at as a curiosity — particularly when you have reason to believe that you and your fathers and their fathers have been wiser about the world than the forebears of the gawkers.

And the Amish have. Considerable reason. Generations before the rest of the country had even begun to realize that there is a question under all the other questions and that our future depends on our ability to answer it, the Amish had faced the question. At a time when we believed, in our trusting innocence, that the cotton gin and the railroad train and the flying machine and the internal combustion engine knew where they were going (and where we were going with them), the Amish had already decided that they weren't joining the procession. And when we accepted the universal, nineteenth-century proposition that the only realistic issue before mankind was the ownership of the means of production, whether by private capital or by the state, the Amish were already firm in their conviction that there is another far more realistic, far more important question: what kind of life mankind will live under any system. Marxists who read Solzhenitsyn now, fifty years after the Bolsheviks took power, are just beginning to understand that such a question might be asked. Free Enterprisers who read Upton Sinclair a generation ago have been aware of it a little longer — and grow more uncertain of the answer every day. We used to laugh at the Amish when they wouldn't buy Model T's. Now we don't even smile. We're too busy trying to get the railroads back in business and keep the Highway Lobby from drowning the continent in concrete.

The fact is that the Amish, for whatever reason, good or bad, lay or religious, had spotted the Idea of Progress for what it was a long time before the rest of us had learned the clichés — or learned in any case that they *were* clichés. It wasn't technological inventiveness or even the miracle of modern science which was going to define the future for the Amish. They themselves would do the defining. And what they would define would be their lives: not the means of life — "means of production" — but the life itself. The life came first and the means afterward. If, to live as they proposed to live, they would have to go without, they *would* go without. Man (they would have said: "man and his immortal soul") was their concern and all the rest an incident: "Modern Improvements," an incident; comfort, an incident.

It is easy enough to dismiss all this as religious aberration — primitivism. What can't be dismissed is the fact that the Amish, for whatever reason, asked the right question: a question we have not been able to bring ourselves to ask even now. We talk about ultimate values. We talk about rearranging our priorities. All we mean is shifting the priority of items in the federal budget — taking a billion or two out of the Pentagon and putting it into housing. What the Amish mean is the nature of human life, the living of human life — everything Metropolis ignores and will go right on ignoring no matter how many miles of condominiums it constructs.

And there is something else the Amish might teach us if, instead of crowding them off their country lanes with our oversize cars, we thought a little more about their history, their lives, their arts. They might teach us what to do about Tom Wicker's Nantucket, about the lost American past which guilty Metropolis-America must not revisit. For the strength of the Amish is precisely that their past is alive in their present. And the greatness of the American past, the unused and wasted greatness which government neglects, and the silent majority ignores, and the young, misled by both, deride, is the fact, unexampled in history, that the American past contains the American future — or would contain it if we, like the Amish, could trust in it again. No nation in history ever announced at its beginning so great a human purpose. That purpose, soiled and bedraggled perhaps, is still around. And not on Nantucket only, or only on a bright clear day.

6

The Ghost of Thomas Jefferson

IT IS A COMMON human practice to answer questions without truly asking them, and the American Bicentennial is merely the latest instance. Everyone knows what the Bicentennial celebrated: the two hundredth anniversary of the adoption, by the Continental Congress, of the Declaration of Independence. But no one asks what the Bicentennial *was* because no one asks what the Declaration *was*. The instrument of announcing American independence from Great Britain? Clearly that; but is that all it was? Was it only American independence from Great Britain we were celebrating on July 4, 1976? – only the instrument which declared our independence? There have been other declarations of unilateral independence from Great Britain (Rhodesia's comes most recently to mind) which no one is likely to remember for two hundred years, much less to celebrate. Just as there are words, including the best-remembered words, in the American Declaration which seem to have more in mind than an American independence from the British crown.

"All men" are said in that document to be created equal and

57

to have been endowed with certain unalienable rights. All governments are alleged to have been instituted among men to secure those rights — to protect them. Are these, then, American rights? Doubtless — but only American? Is it the British government which is declared to have violated them? Unquestionably — but the British government alone? And the revolution against tyranny and arrogance which is here implied — is it a revolution which American independence from the mediocre majesty of George III will win? Or is there something more intended? — something for all mankind? — for all the world?

In the old days when college undergraduates still read history, any undergraduate could have told you that these are not rhetorical questions: that there were, from the beginning, two opinions about the Declaration and that they were held by (among others) the two great men who had most to do with its composition and its adoption by the Congress.

John Adams, who supported the Declaration with all his formidable powers, inclined to the view that it was just what it called itself: a declaration of *American* independence. Thomas Jefferson, who wrote it, held the opposite opinion; it was a revolutionary proclamation applicable to all mankind.

"May it be to the world," he wrote to the citizens of Washington a few days before he died, "what I believe it will be: to some parts sooner, to others later, but finally to all, the signal of arousing men to burst the chains . . ."

And he went on in reverberating words which later and less-honorable revolutionaries have aborted to a different end: "The mass of mankind has not been born with saddles on their backs for a favored few, booted and spurred, ready to ride them by the grace of God."

58

Moreover, these two great and famous men were not the only Presidents of the Republic to choose between the alternatives: A third, as great as either, speaking in Philadelphia at the darkest moment in our history — bearing indeed the whole weight of that history on his shoulders as he spoke — turned to the Declaration for guidance for himself and for his country and made his choice between the meanings.

Mr. Lincoln had been working his way slowly eastward in February 1861 from Springfield to Washington to take the oath of office as President of a divided people on the verge of civil war. He had been making little speeches in city after city as he went, saying nothing, marking time, attempting to quiet apprehensions which his irrelevancies only aggravated. He had reached Philadelphia on the 21st of February where he had been told by the detective, Pinkerton, and by Secretary Seward's son of the conspiracy to murder him in Baltimore as he passed through that city. He had gone to Independence Hall before daylight on the 22nd. He had found a crowd waiting. He had spoken to them.

He had often asked himself, Mr. Lincoln said, what great principle or idea it was which had held the Union so long together. "It was not," he said, as though replying directly to John Adams, "the mere matter of the separation from the mother country."

It was something more. "Something in the Declaration," they heard him say. "Something giving liberty not alone to the people of this country, but hope to the world." "It was that which gave promise that in due time the weights should be lifted from the shoulders of all men."

His hearers seem to have remembered his words in different ways, and it is understandable that they should, for these were private words spoken as much to himself as to them — a speech as moving as a great soliloquy in a tragic play. Anyone else, any modern President certainly, would have said, as most of them regularly do, that his hope for the country was fixed in huge expenditures for arms, in the possession of overwhelming power. Not Mr. Lincoln. Not Mr. Lincoln even at that desperate moment. His hope was fixed in a great affirmation of belief made almost a century before. It was fixed in the commitment of the American people, at the beginning of their history as a people, to "a great principle or idea": the principle or idea of human liberty — of human liberty not for themselves alone but for mankind.

It was a daring gamble of Mr. Lincoln's — but so too was Mr. Jefferson's Declaration — so was the cause which Mr. Jefferson's Declaration had defined. Could a nation be founded on the belief in liberty? Could belief in liberty preserve it? Two American generations argued that issue but not ours — not the generation of the celebrants of the two hundredth anniversary of that great event. We assume, I suppose, that Mr. Jefferson's policy was right for him and right for Mr. Lincoln, because it was successful. The Civil War was won when it became openly and explicitly a war for human liberty — a war to lift the weights from the shoulders of all men. But whatever we think about Mr. Lincoln's view of the Declaration, whatever we believe about the Declaration in the past, in other men's lives, in other men's wars, we did not ask ourselves, as we celebrated its Bicentennial, what it is today, what it is to us.

Our President at the time did not raise the question. The

Congress did not debate it. The state and federal commissions charged with Bicentennial responsibility expressed no opinions. Only the generation of the young, as far as I am informed, so much as mentioned it, and the present generation of the young has certain understandable prejudices, inherited from the disillusionments of recent years, which color their comments.

Tell your children — or, if you prefer, tell my grandchildren — what Thomas Jefferson thought of his Declaration and you will get a blank look with overtones of embarrassment — embarrassment for *you*. Inform them that, in your opinion, Mr. Jefferson's Declaration remains the most profoundly revolutionary document ever published by a responsible people — the only revolutionary declaration ever made on behalf, not of a class or a creed or a special interest of one kind or another but of all mankind, all men, of every man — and you will be told, with courteous amusement, that you have to be kidding.

Express your view that the nation brought into being by that great document was, and had no choice but be, a revolutionary nation, and you will be reminded that, but for the accidental discovery of a piece of tape on a door latch, the President of the United States in the Bicentennial year would have been Richard Nixon. And so it will go until you are told at last that the American Revolution is a figure of obsolescent speech; that the Declaration has become a museum exhibit in the National Archives; and that, as for the Bicentennial, it was a year-long commercial which should have been turned off.

Well, the indignation of the young is always admirable regardless of its verbal excesses — far more admirable, certainly, than the indifference of the elders. But, unfortunately, it is the indifference of the elders we have to consider. And not only because it is a puzzling, a paradoxical indifference, but because it is as disturbing as it is paradoxical.

Does our indifference to the explicitly revolutionary purpose of the Declaration — our silence about Mr. Jefferson's interpretation of that purpose — mean that we no longer believe in that purpose — no longer believe in human liberty? Hardly.

A few years ago we forced the resignation of a President we had just elected by an overwhelming majority because we discovered that he had been engaged in a conspiracy to conceal the truth from us — which means, a conspiracy to obstruct the processes of self-government — which means a conspiracy to suppress our liberties. We then elected, at our next opportunity, a President who made our commitment to human liberty the foundation, not only of his domestic, but of his foreign policy. There can be no doubt, I think, that we in our generation believe in our liberties, in human liberty, in Mr. Jefferson's cause.

But if this is so, if we still believe in the cause of human liberty, why did we celebrate the anniversary of the document which defined it for us without a thought for the meaning of the definition, then or now? Was it because our belief was only a belief, not a purpose, not, at least, a realistic purpose? Was it because, aware of the apparently inexorable conquest of the earth by the most monstrous of all forms of despotism, the modern police state, we had concluded that our Declaration, however inspiring as rhetoric, was only rhetoric?

If we think that, we had better give up thinking. It is true, of course, that the police states, whatever their ideologies (the ideologies no longer matter, only the police), have succeeded in subjugating more than half humanity. They are the new "establishment," the new "existing order."

The Ghost of Thomas Jefferson

But it is also true that there is not a single police state of any ideology which does not confess by its Berlin Walls, its nets of concentration camps, its prison hospitals for the "insane," its censorship of books, its silencing of mouths, its suppression of minds, that it is afraid. And what it is afraid of is precisely the ghost of Thomas Jefferson. Opposition from within, the police state can put down. Wars it can win for a time as Hitler won wars — for a time. But the free man, the free mind, it cannot conquer, it can only imprison, only torture, only kill.

So far, indeed, is Mr. Jefferson's revolution from being obsolete that it is now the one truly revolutionary force in the age we live in. And not despite the police states but because of them. Where the KGB is king the only possible revolution is the revolution of mankind. The revolution of Sakharov, of Solzhenitsyn.

This, then, is the second puzzle, the second paradox, of the Bicentennial. If we still believe in the cause of human liberty for ourselves, as the events of the last years prove we do, and if the cause of human liberty is now the one great revolutionary cause in this inhuman world, as the police states know it is, then why was this greatest of our anniversaries celebrated without a word to start that music in the heart again?

Because we were afraid to affirm our purpose as a people for fear of angering those who have a different purpose? That, I think, is inconceivable. Because we have fixed our minds so long on the menace of the Russian purpose that we have forgotten what our own great purpose was? That is arguable. And the words which would make the argument are three: containment, McCarthyism, and Vietnam — containment abroad, McCar-

63

thyism at home, and Vietnam, as the inevitable consequence of both.

In 1945, when we had driven the Nazis out of Europe and the Japanese out of the Pacific in the name of human freedom and human decency, we stood at the peak, not only of our power as a nation but of our greatness as a people. We were more nearly ourselves, our true selves as the inheritors of Thomas Jefferson and Abraham Lincoln, than we had ever been before. And yet within a few years of that tremendous triumph, of the unexampled generosity of our nuclear offer to the world, of the magnificence of the Marshall Plan, we were lost in the hysterical fears and ignoble deceits of Joe McCarthy and his followers and had adopted, as our foreign policy, the notion that if we "contained" the Russian purpose, countered the Russian initiative, we would somehow or other be better off ourselves than if we pursued our historic purpose as Jefferson conceived it.

The result, as we now know, was disaster. And not only in Southeast Asia and Portugal and Africa but throughout the world. Containment put us in bed with every anti-Communist we could find, including some of the most offensive despots then in business — despots almost as offensive as the Commissars themselves. It produced flagrantly subversive and shameful plots by American agencies against the duly elected governments of other countries. And it ended by persuading the new countries of the postwar world, the emerging nations, that the United States was to them and to their hopes what the Holy Alliance had been to us and ours two hundred years ago.

But bad as all this was, the worst and most destructive effect of this breach of faith, this treason to our own past, was what it did, precisely, to ourselves. It aged us. When I was a young man, sixty years ago, Americans thought of their country as young — thought of the Republic as a nation still at the beginning of its history. A generation later, after the hysteria of McCarthyism and the corrosion of containment, we had become an elderly society huddled over an old man's dream — the dream of "security."

Mr. Jefferson knew, as those who honor him know still, that there is no such thing in human life, no such thing in human history, as what we call "security." He knew that what makes a people great, a nation powerful, is purpose. And what our nation celebrated on July Fourth, 1976 — what it should have celebrated — was precisely the purpose Mr. Jefferson bequeathed to us, the purpose Mr. Lincoln took for answer in his agony.

We are as great as our belief in human liberty — no greater. And our belief in human liberty is only ours when it is larger than ourselves: liberty, as Mr. Lincoln put it, "not alone to the people of this country, but hope to the world." We must become again his "last, best hope of earth" if we wish to *be* the great Republic which his love once saved. We know that. We must say so even now, even toward dark, without a voice to lead us, without a leader standing to come forth. We must say it for ourselves.

PART II

Autobiographical Information

1
Autobiographical Information

❧

EVERYONE KNOWS how it ends — how and more or less when. It's where it began you can't tell. You think of the sixty years and more you've been working and the twenty-odd books of verse on the shelf, the nine plays, eight of them in verse, the six books of prose — all the rest of it. When did it start? That's what the undergraduates are always asking: When did it start? What set you off? How old were you? They want to know for themselves, for their own purposes. How does a man become a writer? Does he just make up his mind to it — decide? Or does something else decide it for him — something he has no part in really? . . . sea change? They can't understand why you won't tell.

When did you decide to be a poet?

You don't decide to be a poet.

Well, become one. When did you become one?

When indeed.

There must have been some moment. Like with Hemingway. You knew Hemingway didn't you? In Paris? He wrote a book about it.

About Paris?

About his happiness in Paris in his early twenties. How he taught himself to write in Paris in the small room in the little hotel with the wet wood in the grate and the pencil sharpener because you wasted pencils with a knife.

He wrote a book about his youth in Paris — about a young man writing in his youth in Paris — learning to write. He was near death when he wrote it. An old man's book about a young man writing — about his work, his wife, his early mornings, the look of the city in those early mornings, the taste of bread, the smell of water . . .

So what does he say about beginning in the book? About the start? The choice? Becoming a writer?

There isn't a word about becoming. The young man in the book is already a writer — the young man as the old man remembers him.

But was he a writer?

The world would say so.

Yes, but *then*. Was he a writer then?

He was twenty-one or -two. He had yet to publish a short story, though he had been writing them, but he had published stories of another kind in the *Kansas City Star* and he was now a foreign correspondent for the *Toronto Star*, a remarkably young, remarkably good, foreign correspondent covering the Lausanne Conference and the rise of Mussolini and the Turkish slaughter of the Greeks in Thrace. It was the pay checks from the *Toronto Star* that provided the little room where he worked and the other rooms where he lived with his wife and later with his wife and son. The old man mentions the checks in passing.

So he wasn't a writer yet. He was a journalist.

70

He had to eat while he taught himself to write.

But even so he wasn't a writer. Not yet.

That was what Gertrude Stein suggested, as the old man remembered with some feeling. Miss Stein believed in serious writers. A serious writer, Miss Stein explained, shouldn't permit himself to be published in newspapers. It didn't look serious. What the young man should do was to resign from the *Toronto Star*. As for eating, supporting his family, making ends meet, he should do what she did — live simply. Miss Stein had a lovely apartment on the Rue de Fleurus, where she lived simply with all those fabulous Picassos purchased at the right time.

So what did Hemingway do?

He was already living simply. He was living above the saw mill, as he called it, on the Rue de Notre Dame des Champs. But, no matter how simply they lived and ate, the ends wouldn't meet as they met for Miss Stein. So he gave up. Not the job with the *Toronto Star* but his life in Paris. They went back to Toronto where he worked full time till his checkbook balanced.

And then?

He resigned from the *Toronto Star*.

Went back to Paris?

Yes, went back to Paris.

And how did he live then?

Went without, the old man says. Went hungry. Borrowed. Borrowed from Sylvia Beach at the bookshop.

So there *was* a moment when he decided to be a writer even if he had to go without — he and his wife and his son.

The old man never mentions a decision: just Gertrude Stein and how the checks stopped coming.

71

But he resigned!

Not to *become* a writer. Not as the old man remembered it. He *was* a writer. He resigned because he *was* a writer — because he had to write.

Even before he had written he was a writer?

Do you remember Cortés on the beaches when he burned his ships? He burned them because he had to go on — because he had heard of Tenochtitlán beyond the mountains. He had never heard of that city before but now he had to go there. He belonged to the journey. Writers belong to the journey. They belong to the work before it is written. That's why they think of themselves as *writers* . . . people who keep on writing . . .

Conversations with the young go something like that but it's no use. They think you're trying not to tell them and they can't understand why you won't. "There must have been a moment . . ."

Well, there was for me but who decided — whether I did, or my wife who wasn't there, or a new moon in a winter sky which was — I can't be certain even now. I know when it happened — a cold, clear, winter evening in February of 1923 when I was five years out of the Great War and four years out of Harvard Law School and trying to support myself and my wife and my two small children by practicing law in a Boston office and teaching a course in Legal Procedure in a night school — trying to find time to write on Saturday afternoons and Sunday mornings when there was a Saturday or a Sunday.

It wasn't Hemingway's situation as he remembered it. I mean I didn't think of myself as a writer *yet*, and certainly not as a poet, and Miss Gertrude Stein had never explained to me how a

serious writer should behave to be considered serious. Indeed I
had never met Miss Gertrude Stein. I was simply a young man,
not so young as I had been once, trying to teach myself to write
better than I had written: a young man who had had a volume
of verses published when he went off to the wars, and now had
another ready, and a publisher willing, but who knew, although
he couldn't have told you why, that something had gone wrong.
I was writing, yes, but out of the margins of my life, and the
work showed it: lines like letters from a brief vacation in another country. And though I had solved, as I thought, the problem of supporting a family and writing verse, I did not *feel* I had
solved anything. If I had, why should I wake at morning with
that sense of *owing?* Owing what? To whom?

I found out that February evening. To go home to Coolidge
Hill in Cambridge from the law office on State Street in Boston
you walked to Park Street Under, took the subway to Harvard
Square and any transportation you could get the rest of the
way — usually your own legs. It took half an hour more or less,
and you made it with your mind on something else — usually,
for me, the witness I'd have on the stand next morning.

That night the ritual changed. When I came out from the
narrow downtown streets to the open Common I saw to west-
ward in the icy sky a new moon waiting — seeming in that
hastening wind to wait. And when I smelled the familiar subway smell, that warm, moist, fetid, daily exhalation, I knew
why. It was for me the moon was waiting. I turned back up the
subway stair, crossed Tremont Street between the inching cars
and headed west across the Common.

I knew my wife would worry. Why wouldn't she? — an
hour by foot — perhaps two hours — I had never walked it.

And yet I had no choice. And not for my sake only but for hers. She had been a singer when I married her — an apprentice singer but not apprentice only. She had studied as a girl in Paris back before the war, learning excitedly and day by day what her voice might be — what it became. One of the loveliest voices of our generation: in the perfection of its tone, the loveliest our generation heard. But now she had her children: the little, blond enquiring boy, the tiny white-haired girl . . . that other on the green grass knoll. She never spoke now of her singing but she sang — at evening — stopping when she heard my footstep: a phrase — Ravel? — a pause to listen — the clear, lifting phrase.

I climbed the Common hill. The moon was waiting still among the bare, black branches, her face turned from me — the slim, silver curve her face made turning in the night away.

Owe! I said. What do I owe? For what? To whom? No one can say I haven't worked, earning my keep in courtrooms before juries, teaching, tutoring . . . whatever — writing when I could take the time to write — first light — night late . . .

Charles Street. The Public Garden. Sidewalks empty in the winter wind. The great black elms on Commonwealth before me. I saw the silver silence through the elm trees.

I understand, I said. It isn't work that matters. It's *the* work — the one work of art. I practice law and teach to make that other possible — to gather time. It isn't true I've wasted time. The war took two years out. There was law school. Teaching erases time by inches. Nevertheless, I have a book now. Not the book I meant to have — I know that. Nevertheless, the book I've written.

Massachusetts Avenue. The long bridge. The wind blows down the Charles. The moon is sinking.

Why do you always turn your face away? I asked the moon. Why do you keep your face turned toward the sun no matter where the sun may lead you? Why do you blind yourself with sunlight?

I was opposite Eliot House when the moon went down. So that was what I'd done . . . had *not* done. I had prepared, provided, made arrangements for a time to come, for work to come, for art to come. There is no art to come: there's only art — the need, the now, the presence, the necessity . . . the sun.

It was the art I owed.

I started up the little path beside the river. Ran. Turned off beyond the Landing. One light in the little house. "Where were you? I've been telephoning . . ." "I know. I have to talk to you. I don't want anything to eat . . ." We talked all night or most of it. She seemed to know what I would say before I'd said it. We made our plans, rose early . . . and the ironies began.

It was not yet nine when I got to the office. I asked to see the senior partner whom I had worked with, loved; was told that he was waiting for me. I walked in. The members of the firm were standing round the room. They had just elected me to partnership . . .

We sailed from Boston to Le Havre late that summer, found a flat in Paris on the Boulevard St. Michel, four floors up, stairs only and no heat but with the Luxembourg across the street behind the roof of the École des Mines and a *bonne's* room up above beneath the tiles where I could do . . . whatever it turned out I *could* do. There had been no scandal, no protest even except the hurt look on the senior partner's face and the insulting letters of a maiden aunt. She had made inquiries in Cambridge and New Haven and had confirmed her own conviction that I had no talent. As for Mr. Edward Arlington Robinson, who had expressed a somewhat different view, he, of course, was merely being kind . . . and not to me but to my publisher to whom he had a certain obligation — something I would come to understand when I grew up.

But my father, with a Scot's respect for the making of books — even of books not made yet — and a brother-in-law's resentment of a sister-in-law's interference in the life of a son, proved perfectly willing to renew the old law-school allowance. (Four can live as cheaply as one . . . in postwar Paris). And as for my wife's father, a Connecticut Yankee like my mother, he generously left unsaid the things he had every right to say but made, I have no doubt, a note for future reference. Only our Cambridge friends spoke out and most of them regarded our departure as a kind of cock-eyed lark appropriate to a cock-eyed generation. Paris? Naturally! Where else would you go but Paris if you were crazy enough to turn down a partnership in the best law firm in Boston to write — what? — *poems?*

But it was no lark to us, either as we headed east out of Boston Harbor on the S.S. *Lafayette,* or as the first Paris winter came on or as the years went by. We had, literally, bet our lives and we knew it. My wife had been eagerly accepted by Nadia Boulanger and was soon singing brilliant little concerts of new songs by composers as old as Satie and as young as Aaron Copland, who was one of Nadia's students, but *my* days under the leaky skylight at 86 Boulevard St. Michel had produced little more than a deeper understanding of the rashness of the wager I had made.

I wrote a few new poems I believed in, some published in T. S. Eliot's *Criterion*, others in Marguerite Caetani's *Commerce*, but most of my time was spent with the work of other writers, reading myself back into the great new channels which had opened in the years before the War and after it — channels which we in the United States had hardly noticed, though two Americans, Eliot and Pound, had played as great a part as anyone in mapping out their course: the Anglo-French connection which brought Rimbaud within reach and the tremendous, almost unimaginable, passage out of China which brought us Tu Fu and Li Po and Po Chü-i.

All this, of course — Rimbaud and Laforgue — the masters of the T'ang — should have been part of any writer's early education but they were no part of mine, and now my only choice was to go back to school — my own school — beneath my skylight. But for how long? How long could I go on reading Yeats — reading Arthur Waley's marvelous translations? — teaching myself enough Italian to *hear* the *Inferno* as I read it? How many months — years — could I give myself? How many years?

We used to laugh about it but not laughing. We would even make mock appointments with each other to meet in Conference to Discuss our Future at four o'clock some afternoon at a little bistro we had never seen off at the other end of Paris. I'd get there first, of course. Her taxi follows. April afternoon. Soft air. Vermouth cassis for one. Pour moi un demi. *You* start. Je vous en prie . . . A hurdy-gurdy on the sidewalk just across. She rises, runs in dance-step down the street. I follow, catch her . . . clinging hands . . .

And then the letters home. She wrote, I couldn't. They were charming letters: Paris days and not a word about the nights between them, nights above our little courtyard side by side, keeping our common secret from each other. When would those twenty lines be written — ten lines even — five — those five lines that would justify . . . ?

Justify what? My burned ships? Hardly. There wasn't a young writer in that city in those years who hadn't burned his ships in one flame or another. No, it was something more that needed justifying. To come to Paris to begin — Paris where Picasso was and Valéry and Stravinsky — was pure effrontery which only work, only unhoped for work, could justify. Paris in the twenties was the last of the great holy cities of the arts. It was Picasso and the changing forms. It was Stravinsky back to conduct the *Sacre* again. It was James Joyce, an Irishman from Trieste with the unpublishable manuscript of a novel which would set the world on fire. It was Alexis Léger of Guadeloupe writing *Anabase* at the Quai d'Orsay, where he was permanent undersecretary, for "St.-John Perse" and all mankind to sign. It was André Masson teasing the surrealistes with the surreality of Verdun. It was Malraux and Aragon and Jules Romains. It was a triumph, a conflagration, of the work of art. And in such a city, at such a time, working is not enough. There must be work accomplished, work beyond your farthest expectation of yourself.

The competitor in Paris in that generation was not some other artist but the limits of the possibilities of art and Marsyas was the hero of the fable — Marsyas who contended with the god and dared to risk the ultimate disaster: "defeated folly flayed among the thorns." Even the youngest writers, painters, seemed to know that. When Hemingway's *In Our Time* was published in the United States and the newspaper critics, those who noticed the book at all, were crossing it off the lists as "juvenile," comparing it to the work of "a small boy who has just decided to become either a great writer or a policeman" — when all this happened, Hemingway, in his loft above the carpenter's shop in the Rue de Notre Dame des Champs with the wood dust floating in the shafts of light, could laugh. He had whittled a new style for his time and he knew it.

And there were others. There was John Dos Passos for example. Dos was in and out of Paris with his Katy in those April years following a road that led, or should have led, from the century of Thomas Jefferson to the century we lived in. Dos with those nearsighted, far, far-seeing eyes had caught the first glimpse of the whole adventure, the vast experience — a view as wide as Whitman's but a century farther on. He had caught the vision of a vision and he came to Paris year by year to find there what he'd lost. Year after year we'd wait for Dos and Katy to turn up for breakfast like two improbable pilgrims, their hands full always of carnations.

And there was Gerald Murphy. Gerald Murphy with his elegant clothes and the house at St. Cloud and the villa on the Cap d'Antibes and his Sara like a bowl of Renoir flowers — Gerald whom the novelists of the Proustian school made use of as material of fiction and who turned out afterward, the decade over and his sons dead and the money all but gone, to have painted some of the most innovative canvases of those years. He too had lived not *in* but *of* the city: not, as his friends thought, for the elegance of graceful living but for the work — the work of art.

And Scott Fitzgerald. Scott Fitzgerald, at the height of his success as a short-story writer, coming back and back to Paris, asking his eternal questions not because he thought the world was made of answers, but because *that* world, he thought, must *know* the answers — even the answer to the question he could never bring himself to ask. Scott with his perfect generosity, his modesty of mind, who knew the questions — all but one.

But it was James Joyce who truly knew what the work demanded of him — James Joyce with his eyes going bad and always, every day, that endless reading, picking the words apart into syllables, twisting the syllables into signposts pointing elsewhere. James Joyce in Adrienne Monnier's flat after her perfect capon and the white, chill wine, saying the Anna Livia Plurabelle for us while our breath caught and our hearts pounded. James Joyce at my wife's piano teaching her Irish songs for a concert — singing the heartbreaking words of *The Brown and the Yellow Ale* in his choirboy's voice, framing the chords with his delicate fingers . . . and then the two of them together, her lovely voice like the flight of a goldfinch, like the curve of light.

These, of course, all but Joyce, were Americans. But they were not in Paris because they were Americans. They were in Paris because it was Paris. And not only the Paris of the damp, sweet-smelling mornings with their flooded gutters and their high-wheeled carts but the Paris of the difficult work — the work of art. They, like all the rest, the young from Africa and the Scandinavian countries and the other America and Britain and the islands of the sea, had made the great improbable decision of the young — the impossible beginning — and it had led them there.

Led them there for what? you say to yourself, remembering. Or you say it to the moon, for there is always a moon left even when you're old if you will only look for it.

Led them there for what? you say. For fame?

Some of them, says the moon. Not many. And how long is fame?

Then why? you ask the moon.

Because the art demanded it.

But if it hadn't?

Then it hadn't.

Harsh alternative!

When were the alternatives of art not harsh? Think of Marsyas flayed among the thorns for his presumption.

Conversations with the moon go on and on. Sometimes sixty years or longer.

2

Art and Law

❦

WHEN I RETURNED to Harvard thirty years after my grad-
uation from the School, not as a professor of law but as
Boylston Professor of Rhetoric and Oratory (which means, being translated out of the Cantabridgian, as Boylston Professor of
Poetry), I was not acclaimed on the steps of Langdell Hall. Instead, I was invited by a series of skeptical law clubs to explain
myself.

The assumption seemed to be that although an ex-*Law Review* editor might reasonably be expected to end up as president
of a bank or head of the Natural Gas Association, he had no
right to turn himself into a poet. Why? I don't know, though I
have often asked. People shuffle their feet and light a cigarette
and look away and you walk back to the Yard wondering if you
really are queer after all.

I don't mean to leave the impression that I am unable to grasp
the difference between the practice of the art of poetry and the
chairmanship of the Gas Association or even a life at the bar. If
I had accepted the partnership in Choate, Hall & Stewart which,
by a lurid coincidence, was offered me on the very day my wife

and I had decided to take her voice and my manuscript and our children to France — if, I say, I had accepted that partnership, I should doubtless possess at this moment a handsome unheatable house in Manchester-by-the-Sea. But it wasn't that kind of difference my young inquisitors in the law clubs had in mind. There seemed to them to be a difference in nature, a difference in worlds, a difference so fundamental that it reflected in some way on the School itself. I shouldn't have gone to the School in the first place if I was capable of turning my back on everything the School represented.

But shouldn't I have gone? And *is* the difference between the law as the School teaches it and poetry as a man pursues it as deep and wide as all that? That there are differences, noticeable differences, between the means of poetry and the means of the law is obvious. Both use words — more or less the same words now that poetry has shuffled off the "poetic" vocabulary which disfigured it in the last century and lawyers have stopped writing as though they were translating themselves out of Latin. But though the words are the same, the tunes are distinguishable. In more senses than one. Lawyers use words as signs standing for meanings whereas poets use them not only as signs but as sounds and as visible objects, as images, as metaphors. I once tried to put this difference into a poem with Robert Frost at one end of the dialogue and that prince of astronomers, Harlow Shapley, at the other. The imagined scene was the Saturday Club, an ancient Boston institution.

AT THE SATURDAY CLUB

Harlow: Our generation discovered the universe.
Robert: That's why we're lost.
Harlow: Men before us

thought in beginnings and ends, all of them.
Nobody knew that time is a circle,
that space is a circle, that space-time
closes the circle.

Robert: They weren't lost.
Harlow: They didn't know they were lost but they were:
they were wrong.
Robert: And we're right and we're lost.
Harlow: When you're right
you can't be lost: you know where you are.
Robert: You know where you are when you're lost.
Harlow: Where?
Robert: Lost.

Poets, you see, are literal-minded men who will squeeze a word till it hurts. Misunderstandings may result. But this does not mean that poets exist in a world of their own or even that they cannot live and breathe in the lawyer's world. Indeed, there are aspects of the lawyer's world which are quite as amenable to a poet's use of words as to a lawyer's. Take for example the legal conception of the corporate entity — the enchanting fiction that a corporation has an existence of its own distinct from the existence of its employees, its officers, and even its owners. When I first met that lovely whimsy in the School I embraced it as though it were mine — much more mine than Bull Warren's or whoever it was who introduced us.

CORPORATE ENTITY

The Oklahoma Ligno and Lithograph Co
Of Maine doing business in Delaware Tennessee
Missouri Montana Ohio and Idaho
With a corporate existence distinct from that of the

Art and Law

Secretary Treasurer President Directors or
Majority stockholder being empowered to acquire
As principal agent trustee licensee licensor
Any or all in part or in parts or entire

Etchings impressions engravings engravures prints
Paintings oil-paintings canvases portraits vignettes
Tableaux ceramics relievos insculptures tints
Art-treasures or masterpieces complete or in sets

The Oklahoma Ligno and Lithograph Co
Weeps at a nude by Michael Angelo.

But little fantasies of this kind have to do not with the fundamental difference alleged to exist between poetry and the law but with the difference in means, the use of words, the way of seeing. Is there such a fundamental difference as my interlocutors of 1949 alleged? Is it true that a man who might be tempted to serve the art should be excluded from the School for the School's sake and his own? Well, let me put a simple — perhaps an over simple — question. What is the business of the law? What would an audience composed of *Law Review* editors, past and present, say was the business of the law? What would the most distinguished of living judges say? The wisest jurist?

I know what one judge would say because he has already said it, though with an uncharacteristic caution: "We who are judges are engaged in part in the study of men." I think I know what a jurist would say, though I should not care to guess at the terms he would use. I am certain I know what this jury of legal editors would find. The business of the law is to make sense of the confusion of what we call human life — to reduce it to order but at the same time to give it possibility, scope, even dignity.

85

But what, then, is the business of poetry? Precisely to make sense of the chaos of our lives. To create the understanding of our lives. To compose an order which the bewildered, angry heart can recognize. To imagine man.

Invent the age, invent the metaphor. Without a credible structure of law a society is inconceivable. Without a workable poetry no society can conceive itself.

For whom — for you or for me or for all of us — were *these* words written?

> *The labor of order has no rest:*
> *To impose on the confused, fortuitous*
> *Flowing away of the world, Form —*
> *Still, cool, clean, obdurate,*
>
> *Lasting forever, or at least*
> *Lasting. . . .*

They come from a poem I wrote for the poet, Wallace Stevens, when he died: a poem which took its metaphor from the ceaseless labor of that tiny architect by whom, life after life, generation after generation, each building on the shoulders of those who went before, the coral reef is raised that calms the water. But this — is it a metaphor which contains *my* life as poet? — *yours* as lawyers? — both?

I have one word more. My education such as it is, began not at Yale, then deep in the blue-sweater era, but in the Law School. I say this not because the occasion demands it (I have said it often and elsewhere), but because it is true. And what was the substance of that education? The Socratic spark which

Art and Law

set insatiable fires where no flame was ever seen before — and
not in my mind only but in many others (I think of my classmate at Yale and in the School — my late and oldest friend,
Dean Acheson). But beyond the spark? Beyond the spark a
vision — the vision of mental time, of the interminable journey
of the human mind, the great tradition of the intellectual past
which knows the bearings of the future. No one, not the most
erudite or scholarly man, who has failed to see that vision can
truly serve the art of poetry or any other art, and by no study
better than the study of the law can the sight be seen. The law
has one way of looking at it. Poetry has another. But the seeing
is the same.

MEN

(on a phrase of Apollinaire)

Our history is grave noble and tragic.
We trusted the look of the sun on the green leaves.
We built our towns of stone with enduring ornaments.
We worked the hard flint for basins of water.

We believed in the feel of the earth under us.
We planted corn grapes apple-trees rhubarb.
Nevertheless we knew others had died.
Everything we have done has been faithful and dangerous.

We believed in the promises made by the brows of women.
We begot children at night in the warm wool.
We comforted those who wept in fear on our shoulders.
Those who comforted us had themselves vanished.

87

We fought at the dikes in the bright sun for the pride of it.
We beat drums and marched with music and laughter.
We were drunk and lay with our fine dreams in the straw.
We saw the stars through the hair of lewd women.

Our history is grave noble and tragic
Many of us have died and are not remembered.
Many cities are gone and their channels broken.
We have lived a long time in this land and with honor.

3

Expatriates in Paris

SOMEBODY ONCE OBSERVED — Yeats for a guess — that the great thing is to survive. I'm not so sure. There may be advantages in outliving one's contemporaries — some of them anyway — but there is little to be said for facing the next generation alone. For the next generation has its questions, too. What was it really like back there? What did all you expatriates *do* in Paris in the twenties?

The worst of it is, if you reply, they don't believe you. If you tell them you never met an expatriate in Paris in six years they smile: They've read the guide book. If you tell them most of the people you knew in Paris in the twenties worked, they smile again: Did you know Fitzgerald? If you say yes, that you knew Fitzgerald, and Hemingway better and longer, and Dos Passos, and Cummings, who was there from time to time, and Wilder on his way through to Rome (which he discovered, characteristically, a generation ahead of the world), and John Peale Bishop, who, in some not unimportant ways, was the most interesting of the lot, and that none of them were expatriates —

if you say all that (which you learn not to) they don't openly tap their heads but you see their fingers twitching. Well, they say at last, did you know Henry Miller? And you give up: No, you never knew Henry Miller, and you excuse yourself and wander off to the nearest elevation from which on a clear day ... You know where *you* will end up in that thesis – a footnote in the bibliography.

No, an idea gets fixed in the collective mind like a loose tooth in a gearbox and you can't get it out. The twenties in Paris were Fitzgerald and soda. Or they were a Lost Generation as Mr. Hemingway said to Miss Stein or Miss Stein to Mr. Hemingway or maybe Miss Toklas to both of them. Or else, and in any event, they were a lot of Americans sitting around in the Dome detesting America – except for those who sat around detesting America in the Rotonde. And the fact that it isn't true – or isn't true, at least, of anyone who mattered – is irrelevant: The notion has deposited itself like stale air on a window – improvisations of beautiful frost through which nothing can be seen.

It's a pity because what was actually happening in Paris in those years – and not only in Paris – was important. What was actually happening was that the arts – including the art of letters – were accomplishing what only rarely in human history they have accomplished as well: They were discovering a profound, and (until they performed their task) unnoticed change in the human situation – the change for which *The Waste Land* and *Ulysses* and the *Cantos* created metaphors; the change which we all now recognize as real, but which no one recognized at all until Stravinsky and Picasso and Eliot and Pound and Joyce and the rest had given it form – forms.

I refer, of course, to the now evident – we would say, self-evident — fact that an age ended with the First World War; that the great voyage of Ulysses — *"Heureux qui, comme Ulysse, a fait un beau voyage"* — had become a Dublin jaunt from morning stool to noisy pub to wife's dishonored bed; that the city of man was now a heap of stones —

These fragments [says Pound of Eliot's *Waste Land*] *you have*
                                                  shelved *(shored)*

What are the roots that clutch [says *The Waste Land*], *what branches*
                                                              grow
Out of this stony rubbish? Son of man,
You cannot say, or guess, for you know only
A heap of broken images where the sun beats,
And the dead tree gives no shelter, the cricket no relief,
And the dry stone no sound of water . . .

To a generation born fifty years after ours all this is part of the canon — its meanings obvious as the meanings of past literature always are. But in the twenties none of it was obvious — even to the professional critics — even to the best of the contemporary critics. There is something strangely (as of now) naive about Edmund Wilson's 1923 review of *The Waste Land* in the *Dial* (the curious review in which he refers to Pound as Eliot's "imitator"):

"And sometimes we feel that he [Eliot] is speaking not only for a personal distress but for the starvation of a whole civilization . . ."

"The starvation of a whole civilization" was a new idea in 1923. A generation born in the century of stability and order — of reliable events, foreseeable consequences — could still, like

Alice through her looking glass, see the old safe world back behind the war: see that *other* room in which chairs were actually chairs, and tables, tables and the sun on the floor, sunlight on the floor. Indeed, to most of us who lived through that war — particularly to the Americans who, so to speak, *went* to the war across an ocean which they expected, with luck, to recross again — to most of us it was assumed as a matter of course that when the war was over we would return to the world we had left.

It was not easy for us — not easy even for a man as perceptive as Mr. Wilson — to accept the fact that that world was no longer there. But Eliot as poet realized it — and created (his duty as poet) the form in which it could be realized by others. Pound realized it — *in* his poem. Dos Passos found fictions which would realize it. And the realization was the age. It was not the Lost Generation which was lost: It was the world out of which that generation came. And it was not a generation of expatriates who found themselves in Paris in those years but a generation whose *patria*, wherever it may once have been, was now no longer waiting for them anywhere.

That realization produced two consequences: *The Waste Land* and the forms in which the waste land was discovered. The twenties were not only the years of the images of the collapse of Christendom and the drowning of Cleopatra's barge and the end of an age. They were also high-hearted — even high-handed — years of innovation, arguably the greatest period of literary and artistic innovation since the Renaissance. The burden of the song may have been tragic, but the song itself was new and then new again and then even newer, as though, precisely because the bottom had fallen out of the historical tradition, a new ship had to be built for every voyage to sea. Indeed — and this is perhaps the most significant fact about the period — the avant-garde was composed in those years not, as ordinarily, of the frustrated and defeated but precisely of the principal figures of the time. Joyce was avant-garde (though he would have rejected the designation). Stravinsky was avant-garde. Picasso was avant-garde for generations. With the result that the surrealists, who had announced, by manifesto, their right to head the procession never got far enough forward to hear the drum.

It is these two characteristics, surprisingly combined, which make the quality of the time: the shimmer and sheen of the inventiveness and the tragic depth of the theme. Art, with the great figures of the decade, was accomplishing what art exists to accomplish — and accomplishing it with freshness and vividness and courage: It was recreating with new means — almost with a new vocabulary — the metaphors for our experience of our lives, the tragedy of our experience. Not philosophy, not the church, but painting and poetry and music showed us what and where we were.

4
Moonlighting on Yale Field

&

CONVENTIONAL WISDOM notwithstanding, there is no reason either in football or in poetry why the two should not meet in a man's life if he has the weight and cares about the words. I know a large young professor at Brown who has three books of verse and a career in the professional leagues to his credit and who looks and sounds entirely believable in both parts. As I put it at the time:

> *He keeps the door to windward open so*
> *he'll know when it blows.*
> *He knows it when it blows.*
> *He knows*
> *it.*
> *   When it blows he*
> *knows.*

My own situation is somewhat different from Michael Harper's. He must be close to six foot six and two hundred and twenty pounds whereas I have never been able to grow beyond five foot ten and a hundred and sixty-five. However, Yale teams of the years before the First World War were no more professional in their statistics than in anything else and a man could survive at a hundred and sixty-five if he kept moving.

Also, it was relatively easy to avoid detection. The football squad didn't read the *Yale Literary Magazine* and those who did never went to the games. Actually I was well along in my seventy-eighth year before public attention was directed to my youthful moonlighting on Yale Field, but when it happened I was faced with a rather embarrassing situation, because the public attention came from the National Football Foundation and Hall of Fame which wanted to give me an award, while the ghost of Johnny Mack kept saying No.

Johnny Mack was the trainer of Yale teams in the first years of the century and he knew, none better, which of his charges was entitled to a football award and, more to the point, which wasn't. His estimate of my claims had been conveyed to me in the fall of my sophomore year in eleven soft but distinctly audible Irish syllables at the close of an afternoon of disastrous practice. As we bumped back to the old gym on Elm Street in the chartered trolley car which served us as combination dressing room and transportation, Johnny Mack nudged me, directed his sad gaze out over the squalid western purlieus of New Haven and remarked: "You'll be lucky to make the training table."

Anyone who has heard tales of the Yale football training table in those years will relish the insult. As for me, the smart was still fresh in the wound after more than fifty years when the National Football Foundation wrote me; but that didn't prevent me from showing up at the Waldorf in December of 1969 and addressing the flower of American football there assembled. I suppose it was because the conventional wisdom about the relation of the most violent of games to the most human of the arts had always annoyed me, but, whatever the reason, I exorcised the ghost of Johnny Mack by reminding the all-Americans of the famous remark of my classmate and beloved friend, Dean Acheson, when accepting an award for public service from a Milwaukee organization which hated his guts. "It is the honors we don't deserve," said the Secretary of State, "we accept most gratefully."

And, that confession made, however vicariously, I went on to say my say about the taste of blood and lime on an autumn afternoon — a taste which is as much a part of the delight of being alive as anything else on earth.

I had only one glorious memory of my football years, I told them, and its setting was neither Yale Field in New Haven nor Soldiers Field in Cambridge, but the bar at the Tremont Hotel in Boston after the freshman game of 1911. We — we being the Yale Freshman Team — had just held the best Harvard Freshman Team in a generation (Brickley, Bradlee, Hardwick, Coolidge, Logan) to a nothing-nothing tie in a downpour of helpful rain and we were relaxing, not without noise, when the coach of that famous Harvard Freshman Team approached us, looked us over, focused (he had had a drink or two himself) on me and announced in the voice of an indignant beagle sighting a fox that I was, without question, the dirtiest little sonofabitch of a center ever to visit Cambridge, Massachusetts. It was heady praise. But unhappily I didn't deserve that honor either: I was little but not *that* little.

I told them this, I explained, to propitiate, if it was at all possible, the wholly understandable feelings of those in the room who had run into poets before in situations in which they couldn't avoid them (a reception, say, at their wives' clubs before a lecture they couldn't get out of) and who saw no reason why they should have to meet one on their own ground in their time off. And with that, I took the offensive:

The truth is, gentlemen, that this game of yours (I will not call it *ours*) has powers of which even you have never dreamed. It can not only turn poets into so-and-sos: it can turn them (which is not necessarily the same thing) into Assistant Secretaries of State. It has, indeed, on one recorded occasion, done so. During the Second World War my nomination to that office was before the Senate Committee on Foreign Relations, on the motion of President Roosevelt, and I was there with it to be questioned in the usual way. Except that the usual way turned out to be anything but usual. At the end of a long day devoted to my views on Franco and de Gaulle and Chiang Kai-shek and Colonel McCormick of the *Chicago Tribune* (whose views on me were public knowledge), the session was about, or so I hoped, to adjourn when Bennett Champ Clark of Missouri tiptoed in with a small book in his hand which had, to me, an uncomfortably familiar look. The Chairman recognized him with a nod. Did he wish to be heard? Well, yes, he did, now that the Chairman mentioned it. He wished to ask Mr. Mac-Leish a question. And he opened the little book to the page marked by his finger and began to read. It was, of course, a poem. Worse still it was a poem by me. Worse even than that it was a poem by me on the subject of love — and the Senator from Missouri, reading with what the Supreme Court once called "all deliberate speed," allowed that fact to soak in. When he had finished he glanced sardonically in my direction, turned to the Chairman and announced that he would be interested to know whether Mr. MacLeish regarded the author of *that* as qualified to serve as an Assistant Secretary of *State* of the United States of *America* at the crucial point of a World *War!*

I could think of no wholly responsive answer, and there might well have been a long and awkward pause punctuated by the snickers of the Press had it not been for the astonishing memory and brilliant sense of total irrelevance of Happy Chandler of Kentucky. "Mr. Chairman," said Senator Chandler, "I also have a question for Mr. MacLeish if the Senator will yield. I should like to ask him if he did not play football at Yale." The room relaxed. The Press stopped snickering. The Chairman rose. And that, so far as I am aware, was all the answer Bennett Champ Clark of Missouri ever got.

I do not suggest that football was regarded by the Senate Committee on Foreign Relations as an antidote for poetry. The Committee (I have profound respect for the Senate of the United States) understood that poetry has no need of antidotes being itself the most powerful of all antidotes for the most grievous of all human ills — human mortality. But poetry is one thing and men who write poems are another and no Senate Committee with a proper respect for the political future of its members would willingly confirm for public office a man who was known to perpetrate poems *unless* there were ameliorating circumstances. Football was the ameliorating circumstance in my case. And it is that fact which provides the text for the brief sermon I am about to preach. You can put the text in the form of a question.

What is there about the game of football — about the mere

fact of having played the game of football — which permitted that Senate Committee on Foreign Relations to adjourn in peace? What guarantee does football offer that a man who has played the game, whatever else he may do or be, will at least *act* as though he were human?

Or put the same question in present rather than historic terms? Why do men, as busy as most of you, take time to spend an evening such as this? Why does a man as old as I, living a couple of hundred miles back in the hills, drive through rain and snow and sleet to *talk* at such an evening? What moves us all? Why are we haunted by the smell of torn earth and winter grass and the taste of time?

I think I know and I think you know too. There are some things in life which have a poignance which does not belong so much to them as to the human circumstances which surround them — to the fact that they are *common* human experiences — experiences *in* common.

War is one. No decent man ever fought a war without hating it. But, at the same time, no decent man ever lived through the fighting of a war who did not remember, all his life long, the deep, almost inexplicable, satisfaction of the common struggle, the common risk.

I tried once to find words for this in a poem about *my* generation's war — what is now called, ironically, the *First* World War. With the permission of the shade of the late Senator from Missouri I should like to say a few lines:

Why are the old soldiers brothers and nearest?

For this: with their minds they go over the sea a little and find themselves in their youth again as they were in

Soissons and Meaux and at Ypres and those cities.

A French loaf and the girls with their eyelids painted
bring back to aging and lonely men
their twentieth year and the metal odor of danger.

It is this in life which, of all things, is tenderest —
to remember together with unknown men the days
common also to them and perils ended.

Now football, of course, is far from war — modern war in any case. But its poignance is that same poignance. In football as in war, it is true, as my poem puts it, that:

The brotherhood is not by the blood certainly,
but neither are men brothers by speech, by saying so:
Men are brothers by life lived and are hurt for it.

It is this that we know together in this room, all of us, of all ages. We have all *played* this magnificent, wild, extravagant, difficult and often dangerous game — *played* it, not merely watched it *being* played on a small screen in a hot parlor on a Sunday afternoon. We know the feel of it, the desperate excitement, the triumph, the despair — above all the sense of those others *with* us who know it also — feel it as we feel it. It is this which gives the game its power over our memories and minds — a power which those who have never played find inexplicable — even incredible.

And it is this too which gives the game something more than its power over us — which gives it its potential importance in our troubled society, and particularly in that part of our society where the troubles are the troubles of the young. For one of the deepest troubles of the young in the world we live in is precisely the loss, the lack, of that sense of common undertaking, common risk — the loss, the lack, of the deep delight of the common labor.

Unlike a great many of my aging contemporaries I have the greatest admiration for this generation of new Americans. They care deeply about the world, about mankind. They have profound, if not always articulate, misgivings about the direction human life on this planet, including American life, is taking. They are, to borrow that wonderful old Quaker verb, "concerned." They have hope. They have convictions. But all this is undercut and somehow crippled by a curious mood, a sense of loneliness, even of helplessness — of isolation — "alienation" is the fashionable term. Those of you who have teen-age children or grandchildren and who keep up with the new movies, the new plays, the new songs — above all the new songs — which appeal to this new generation know what I mean. You know the mood. And, knowing it, you must have reflected often, as others also have reflected, on its meaning for the future of this Republic. For nothing, surely, can be more dangerous to a democracy, to a *self*-governing people, than precisely this sense of individual separation, impotence, aloneness — alienation.

I am not so fatuous as to suppose that a college game — or what used to be a college game before it became the greatest of television spectaculars — can change the mood of a troubled generation. But neither am I able to forget that that same mood of isolation and loneliness existed in *our* youth also and that many in our generation found in football that precise sense of participation, of common labor, which has changed the lives of many in this room — a sense which nothing — not even time itself — not even fifty-seven years of time — can take away.

In a technological age, when there are not many ways in the ordinary course of life itself to learn the profound meaningfulness of common undertaking — not many opportunities, for example, to raise a barn by calling in the neighbors — in a technological age a game such as yours may be one of the few remaining means to that most essential wisdom. And though not every man *can* play football, or would want to if he could, the potential power of the game may still be greater than the inexperienced would suppose. To keep a human understanding alive, to teach a human lesson, not every man needs to learn it at first hand. As long as the experience persists — as it persists here — the *idea* will survive. And it is the survival of the idea which counts.

5

A Lay Sermon for the Hill Towns

LAY SERMONS SHOULD BE satisfied with lay texts. I have
taken mine from a letter written in the town of Conway,
Massachusetts, on the seventeenth day of July in the year 1892.
It was written by my grandmother, Julia Whittlesey Hillard,
whose husband, my grandfather, was, in that year, the newly
settled pastor of the Conway church, having previously served
in a sequence of churches beginning at Hadlyme near the mouth
of the Connecticut River in the 1850s and ending, forty years
later, here in the Hoosac Hills, looking out over Deerfield and
the narrowing valley.

I mention this migration because it has a good deal to do with
my grandmother's letter. Most parsons stay more or less put
once they have found a congregation, but not Elias Brewster
Hillard. My grandfather was the son of a sea captain in the
North Atlantic trade and he had inherited the habits of the
quarterdeck: he not only spoke out; he spoke out in the wind's
teeth. When the Civil War came along he found himself in a
milltown in Connecticut where uniforms were manufactured for

the Union armies, most of them shoddy. The millowner was, of course, a deacon of the church, and placed, as such, in a conspicuous seat where my grandfather's sermon on shorn lambs could reach him. The result was foreseeable though not necessarily foreseen: the Hillard family moved on in the predestined direction — north, away from the prosperous communities and fashionable churches, bringing its growing brood of children and an ever-increasing reputation for candor.

It was my grandmother, of course, who suffered from all this, though she never said so even to herself. She was a small woman, delicately made, who had borne nine children in almost as many towns and who had paid at last with her own health for her endless labors at the laundry tub and the stove and the sink and the broom, to say nothing of her duties in the church and the Sunday School and the sickrooms of the many towns. Five years before the wanderers came to rest in Conway she had been ill, and if she was now recovered it was not because her life had changed but because Conway, she thought, had healed her with its hill-town air, its hill-town sun, and its northwest wind out of Vermont and the Adirondacks. The letter of July 17, 1892, was about that miracle.

She had been corresponding all her adult life with a beloved teacher. "Dear Miss Guilford" had not heard of Conway, Massachusetts, and must be told at length in a Sunday letter. "I reserve," my grandmother wrote, "the more leisurely writing-time that Sunday brings as my own and to spend at my own sweet will." Which was gallant enough in a little lady who never had time of her own — but which proved, before she had written her way down the first, brief page, to be overly optimistic. She caught herself, as she put it, "nodding" and went off to get her aged mother to bed, after which she decided to finish her never-finished washing and go to bed herself — "and what a good harbor that is when night comes."

But the letter was still a Sunday letter when she went on with it — Sunday the 24th of July instead of Sunday the 17th. And the subject was still the same. Dear Miss Guilford must imagine this Conway she has never seen. And what is she to imagine? Conway people in this generation will be surprised. She is to imagine Arcadia. "That," my grandmother writes, "is the name by which we know it." And where does Arcadia begin? Back of the little parsonage which still stands where it stood then — halfway up the hill that climbs south out of the village street. "The houselot is a very large one with much of hill and dale in it, and a bird's nest of a house amidst the trees and shade (not too much, however; the sunshine pours in on every side)." And off she goes, dragging Miss Guilford almost literally by the hand.

My grandmother had never heard, I suppose, of Emily Dickinson. Nobody had in those days, not even within thirty miles of Amherst. And yet there is an echo in her words of that childlike voice with its unchildlike meanings — "You come with me in at the large gateway and up the rising, slightly winding, path to the little house with its porches and vines and flowers — past that and past the garden on its high terrace to your right, and past the dull red barn on your left, and up a grassy path through a shady orchard with all the time such lovely views opening before and around you that you pay no heed to the way by which you came but feel, when here, that you have been translated and know a new heaven and a new earth." And so the journey goes on, my grandmother running ahead and dear Miss Guilford following after as best she can. "Here we are at the top of a steep, grassy, wooded hill sloping to the village. This is Arcadia."

But not *all* of Arcadia as it turned out. There was something more — a healing something which had saved her from "that long and fearful illness . . . Conway with its tonic air and its simple, wholesome affectionate life has worked wonders for me. And how devoutly thankful I am! For it means so much — and not to me alone, but to all my precious family and to our dear people . . . I prize my new strength very highly and I try to make a conscience of guarding it."

But even this last and deeply personal confession was not enough. There was something more that had to be said, had to be shown. "I wish I had a camera that could take a picture of Conway life for you. It is a busy little place with four churches — Congregational and Methodist and Baptist, yes, and Catholic — very earnest, warm-hearted Christians, intelligent, intellectual, spiritual, ready for every good work, appreciative and responsive. Our life and work here are more a labor of love than in any of the homes yet. And I do believe we were never loved as we are here, or had so fruitful a field of service before. And is that not wonderful when you consider the ages we have come to? I am 57!"

Arcadia indeed — more than Arcadia — a good and healing life in a very human community sustained by the earth and the streams and the sun and the labor that belongs to a land of little valleys and great shouldering hills. But that was 1892 when my grandmother was fifty-seven and I had just been born a thousand miles away in Illinois. And where are we now? My grandmother is long dead and I am eighty-four, and the town . . .

there are those who believe that the town too is close to the end of things: close to the loss of its identity as a town like so many of those famous settlements below us in the valley which have dissolved into the endless anonymity of subdivisions and expressways. Where is Hatfield now? An exit on Route 91. Where does Amherst begin? Where a white post on Route 9 tells you you are "Entering Amherst."

Well, it is always possible, I suppose, that the hill towns will disappear in the same way: turn into bedroom towns which will turn into rural slums which will be "restored" by public housing in which no one would willingly live. It is possible, but it is not inevitable. And the reason it is not inevitable is the reason my grandmother discovered as she led Miss Guilford to Arcadia. A town is not land, nor even landscape. A town is people living on the land. And whether it will survive or perish depends not on the land but on the people; it depends on what the people think they are. If they think of themselves as my grandmother thought of the people of Conway in 1892, if they think of themselves as living a good and useful and satisfying life, if they put their lives first and the real estate business after, then there is nothing inevitable about the spreading ruin of the countryside. The hill towns will survive as long as they are inhabited by people who think of themselves as living their own lives, think of their neighbors as people who will keep the fields open and the woods green and the little rivers running for their lives' sake, and for the sake of human life.

Economic inevitability is not only Marxist dogma. It is also, and increasingly, American fantasy. To preserve something for life's sake when money can be made by destroying it is sentimental to the American business mentality, and the American business mentality is now established as the norm of American thinking. My grandmother would not have agreed, and it's no use trying to dispose of my grandmother by throwing words like "sentimental" at her memory. No woman who bore nine children in as many parsonages, and then brought them up on a minister's stipend, cooking and washing and sewing for the lot, was ever sentimental or could afford to be. Women like that were far more practical than real-estate operators. And what they were practical about was human values: the kind of thing the real estate developer has never thought of. "Development pays, doesn't it?" says the developer. Yes, it pays, sometimes, but what does it do to life in the town? says my grandmother. "Life in the town!" says the developer. "Let them watch television!" Which wouldn't mean much to my grandmother but might mean something to some of us.

No, the crisis in the American hill towns is not a hill-town crisis. It is an American crisis. Sooner or later, and sooner rather than later, the country people, the practical mothers and grandmothers, are going to have to challenge the business mentality which turns land into real estate and small towns into dispensable relics of the past which developers can exploit for profit. They are going to have to teach the impractical and sentimental business mentality what a town actually is: what one town was to Julia Whittlesey Hillard — a place where she was made whole, where her life was recreated, a place of which she could say: "Our life and work here are more a labor of love than in any of the homes yet. And I do believe we were never loved as we are here." That is practical talk. It puts first things first. It means something.

6
Remarks on the Pulitzer Prize

Ӭ

COLUMBIA UNIVERSITY has decided, after fifty years of distributing Pulitzer Prizes, to pause,

> *Draw rein, draw breath,*
> *Cast a cold eye*
> *On life, on death . . .*

and take stock of the consequences. And *we* are the consequences. We are Mr. Pulitzer's dream made flesh. We are the men and women who were chosen. What have the chosen to do on the great day, at the solemn appraisal, the ultimate assize? What, to put it crudely, can they conceivably *say?*

Barbara Tuchman has a story in her *Proud Tower* which illuminates our predicament. It seems that the father of Richard Strauss, a famous virtuoso of his day, was asked how he would prove his right to be considered the foremost living performer on the horn. "I don't," he said. "I don't prove it. I admit it."

Conceivably we might follow the Strauss example, but I

doubt if we will. The trouble is that our emotions are engaged in a way in which the emotions of the egregious horn player apparently were not. We can't merely *admit* the charge against us. We are proud of it. As our presence here this evening proves.

And it is there, of course, that the ambiguity of which I speak appears — the embarrassment. Of what, precisely, are we proud? Of ourselves? Of our certification by a great university as superior performers on our various instruments?

Possibly. Poets — I will confine myself to poets leaving the novelists, journalists, playwrights, composers, historians, biographers to speak for themselves — poets are at least as human as anyone else. Not to say more so.

And possibly it is only ourselves we are proud of. But I doubt it. For poets, though they may know only too well how to value themselves, know how to value something else even more. They know how to value poetry — poetry past, present, and to come.

And their real pride, therefore, consists not in being preferred to their contemporaries — they know how often those preferences are reversed by time and how frequently the forgotten poet of one age is the remembered of another — but in feeling themselves a part, however small a part, of that timeless, continuing, and inextinguishable pulse of life which poetry is.

What these awards have done for many in this indifferent world of ours — this particularly indifferent American world — is somehow to *include* them. We do not all of us have the courage, as we certainly do not have the reasons, which made it possible for Keats to say, at the loneliest moment of his life, that he knew he would be among the English poets at his death. We need, most of us, a sign of recognition. Not recognition of our ultimate worth as poets — only poetry itself can give that — but recognition that we exist. That we are there. Among those who went before and those who will come after.

To pick up, in your forty-third unanswered year, the copy of the *Paris Herald* which says you have a Pulitzer Prize is not to be proud of yourself. It is to think of Edwin Arlington Robinson whom you revere, and Robert Frost whom you will learn to, and the others in your own generation whom you have heard of and never known, and all the rest still younger, still to come.

No one believes, least of all the perceptive president of the university which gives these prizes, that the Pulitzer Prizes will change the art of letters in America; art is not impressed by awards. But there are many who have received them who will testify that nothing in their lives made life as possible — made work as grateful — as the moment when they learned this honor had been given *them.*

PART III

Dramatis Personae

1

The Venetian Grave

THE OBLIGATION of the living to the dead, as the old Greeks
knew, is to cleanse the corpse with fire before covering it
with earth. "Burn me in my armor," says the shade of Elpenor
to Odysseus, "and make a mound for me on the shore of the
gray sea in memory of an unhappy man." We should remember those words when we think of Ezra Pound in his Venetian
grave.

If ever a dead man needed living men to help him, it is Pound;
and if ever a living generation risked misfortune in the failure to
perform its duty, it is ours. The dead go on and on in time with
the rest of us, and unless they go honestly, unless they go as
themselves, as what they really are, we may all be led astray.
Think of the ghost of John Keats. For almost a century after
that mawkish epitaph was carved into the stone above his head
in the Protestant Cemetery in Rome, English poetry and Western thought were haunted by a fraudulent impostor whose voice
can still be heard in the sniveling contemporary notion that life
is a brutal joke and man its helpless victim and poetry his feeble

and self-pitying cry. John Keats, a brave and honest maker, had been misburied.

And so has Ezra Pound, though in a different way. Keats suffered at the hands of others: a generation of unusually stupid critics and a group of friends more fatuous than the friends of poets usually are. Pound, though he has not lacked for stupid critics, suffered not at the hands of others but at his own. It was he himself who invented the dead man who survives him. Where the body carried down the dark canals should have been that of a great and innovative poet, it was instead the body of a man once tried for treason; a man who had defended fascism in strident public broadcasts at the very moment when that unspeakable beastliness had all but conquered the continent of Europe; a man whose name was associated with the most idiotic literary squabble of the age — in brief, the man the television cameras and the newspapers remembered. And that man, though not the truth of Ezra Pound, was Pound's creation.

It is this fabricated man — this "mask," to use the fashionable term — we must examine if we wish to do our duty by the dead and by ourselves. Ours is an age, particularly in the United States, when fraud has become a form of government. Fraud and government may exist together but not fraud and art. We can perhaps survive a ruler who deceives us but not a poetry that lies. And Pound, whatever else he may have been, was unarguably a poet. Was he also, then, a traitor?

The answer to that is certain — one of the few self-evident certainties in a cloud of doubt. Pound was brought to trial for treason — for attacking the policy and conduct of his own government on the official radio of a country with which his country was at war — and the constitutional question at the threshold was whether his admitted words and actions constituted the crime with which he was charged. It was a crucial question, given the guarantee of freedom of speech in the First Amendment, but Pound's lawyer decided not to contest the case on that issue but to enter a plea of not guilty by reason of insanity. That plea prevailed, but events were shortly to prove the decision wrong in law, however right it may have been in expediency.

Twenty-odd years later, toward the end (if it was the end) of the Vietnam War, a former attorney general of the United States did in Hanoi precisely what Ezra Pound had done in Rome. He attacked the policy and conduct of his own country in the capital of a country with which the United States was at war, and though he did not use the North Vietnamese electronic system to broadcast his charges, the effect on world opinion was the same and far more serious. And yet this former attorney general, though the then government of the United States detested him personally and abhorred his views, was neither tried nor indicted nor even arrested. And for the good and sufficient reason that the right to dissent, the right to criticize, had by then been exercised in time of war by so large a majority of the American people that if wartime criticism was treason, the Republic itself would have had to be indicted.

But if the mask of Ezra Pound as traitor is a lying mask, if his indictment by the Department of Justice was an error of law and his attorney's plea of insanity an error in tactics and his incarceration in St. Elizabeth's a miscarriage of justice, what shall be said of the second mask this dead man wears? If he was not a traitor, was he, as is constantly said, a fascist? That he was an admirer of the Fascist government of Italy is obvious. That he was often anti-Semitic is only too clear. That he never protested against the nasty little triumphs of Mussolini in Ethiopia and Spain or the monstrous behavior of Hitler in Germany or even the Gestapo terror and torture in Paris — that he never protested against any of this (only against the decision of his own country to put a stop to it) is sadly true. But was he a fascist? Certainly he never thought he was. He thought of himself as his books prove, as an old-line American Jeffersonian, a believer in the American Republic as its founders conceived it, and though his notions of that Republic would have astonished Mr. Jefferson, Mr. Adams, and Mr. Franklin, there is no reason to doubt that he honestly held them. He was even able to find common bonds between Mussolini and Jefferson and to relate the Social Credit notions of his friend Major Douglas to the economic history of the United States.

In the old Red-hunting days of Senator Joe McCarthy, American newspapers used to talk about "conscious" Communists, "card-carrying" Communists. Certainly Pound was never a fascist of either variety. But how then are the Roman broadcasts to be explained? Quite simply, I think, by that peculiar naiveté which is the occupational disease of intellectuals: that infatuation with ideas at the expense of experience which compels experience to conform to bookish preconceptions. Pound was widely if not deeply read, but his experience of the world was thin. His own country he knew only through the veil of print — largely historical print. Having spent all his adult life abroad, he knew nothing of the crucial American decades from 1914 on: the disillusionment that followed the First World War, the cynicism and shoddiness of the twenties, the agony of the Great Depression, the social revolution that followed, the grim decision forced on the country by the rise of Hitler.

And the same thing was true in other terms of the European countries in which he lived during those years. He adjusted the facts to his theories. He read but did not see. Insofar as fascism fitted his preconceptions he admired it: What did not fit he merely ignored. By the time of the Roman broadcasts he must have been the only intelligent man left in Europe who did not understand what a Nazi conquest of the world would mean to art and human decency and everything else he loved, including civilization itself. Which means, not that he was himself a fascist, but simply that he was an intellectual capable of the intellectual's characteristic mistakes: a total misreading of his own time. Like his own Hugh Selwyn Mauberley, he was "wrong from the start," but not, as in Mauberley's case, for aesthetic reasons. Rather for personal reasons: wrong as a human being. Any man who could make a religion of Social Credit in the lifetime of Adolf Hitler, and fix his mind on usury as the key to the world's ills at a moment when the writers and artists of Paris were being tortured and executed for their addiction to human liberty must be written down as childish, to put it as kindly as possible. And when that same man goes on in the same lifetime of this same Adolf Hitler to equate usury with the Jews — to make the Jews a symbol of the crime of usury — the naiveté becomes something else and worse: unspeakably worse. To be wrong is a fault in a poet as in anyone else — worse in a poet because a poet's business is to see truly — but to be wrong, even to be monstrously wrong, is not the same thing as to be a fascist, and Pound, at least in his death, is entitled to the distinction.

But there is a third mask in addition to the fascist jowl and the traitor's smirk: the literary domino bestowed by the great fracas that followed the award to Pound of the Bollingen Prize while he was still incarcerated in St. Elizabeth's Hospital in Washington. This mask can only be examined in the light of its history. What happened, briefly, was that a group of his friends, including a number of the most distinguished American poets of the time, conceived the idea of a new national prize for poetry to be awarded by the Library of Congress through a jury of notables who would select Pound as the first recipient, thus dramatizing his situation and putting the government, and particularly the Department of Justice, in an awkward if not untenable position. The Soviet Union had not, at that time, begun the use of mental institutions to silence artists and intellectuals, but the possibilities of such a practice were evident even then. The conscience of mankind would, it was hoped, take fire.

And it did, but not the fire hoped for. The excited reaction came not from the defenders of human liberty but from the patrioteers of what Mr. Nixon was to call the Silent Majority. And the issue raised was not the justice of Pound's incarceration but the justice of the award of a national prize to a man indicted for treason. No one had realized how many poetry societies there were in the Republic until the Bollingen Prize was established, nor how many of their members held views not only about the art but also about its relation to such academically unfashionable attributes as virtue. A New York critic of the time would rather have gone unpublished than discuss the relation of a poet's work to his merits as a man, but innumerable letters to the editor began to argue precisely that position in small newspapers and large across the country, and the general conclusion was fairly unanimous.

The Venetian Grave

It was that unexpected opinion which brought the deluge. Critics and intellectuals, particularly those who thought of themselves as constituting the avant-garde, rushed to the defense of Pound in a roar of rage. Excellence in poetry, they informed the yokels, had nothing to do with right-mindedness or morality or patriotism or anything else but excellence in poetry. A criminal or a pervert, a pimp or a pederast, could be as good a poet as John Milton and probably better, and as for fascism, look at D'Annunzio! Nothing very intelligent was said about the reasons for all this, nor did anyone ask where it left the art of poetry — whether poetry was so totally inconsequential that it made no difference what it said — but the effect was overwhelming. And so was the harm to Pound. No one bothered to find out what Pound thought: It was simply taken for granted that he must believe in an aesthetic that would justify his political aberrations, a poetry to which the human world, the moral world, the historical world, is irrelevant. And the consequence was that the dead man who was carried down the dark canal became, in addition to everything else, a dilettante.

Of all the lying masks, this, of course, is the most palpably fraudulent. Pound was one of the inventors of modern poetry: in retrospect, one must say, the principal inventor. And modern poetry, which is still the poetic achievement of the century, is a poetry committed to the human world, to the historical world, the moral world, as Yeats's work after *Responsibilities* proves and Eliot's *Waste Land* and Perse and Neruda and Seferis and the rest of those enduring names, with Pound's not last or least. The nearest thing we have, either in prose or verse, to a moral history of our tragic age is the *Cantos* of Ezra Pound, that descent, not into Dante's hell, but into ours. And the greatest contribution our century has made to the enrichment of the tradition of poetry is the translation of that most human poetry, the Chinese: a work in which Pound played a useful and influential part. To bury this man as a dilettante is a distortion indeed.

So we are left at the end, as so often in tragic life, with a dilemma. We can burn Pound's bones clean of the taint of treason and clean of the reek of dilettantism, but the flaw of the Roman broadcasts still remains. There is no use pretending, as some still do, that Pound was insane when all that happened. The *Pisan Cantos* were written afterward, and it was in those later years that he himself saw clearly where the fault had been. He was not mad in any meaningful sense of the word when he ranted on the Fascist radio, though he was deluded: deluded on the central issue of his time. His fame must suffer for it, as he suffered. But the suffering should be just. The Venetian grave holds neither dilettante nor traitor but, like Elpenor's, a foolish and unhappy man . . . who was a poet also . . . a master poet for whom a mound should now be raised on the shore of the gray sea.

2

Gerald Murphy

IN THE TEN YEARS since his death, the American painter
Gerald Murphy has achieved a considerable fame for reasons
having nothing to do with his work or even with the art he prac-
ticed. He is an object of interest because he lived in Paris at a
time when, retrospectively, living in Paris was the thing to do
and because, while other Americans lived there meanly or without imagination, he lived there well. His house at Saint Cloud
was Gounod's old house, above the railroad cut, with a view of
Montmartre through the snow. His friends were the principal
men of the twenties — Picasso and Stravinsky and Fernand
Léger and, among the Americans, Dos Passos and Hemingway
and sometimes Fitzgerald. He was the first summer-resident of
Cap d'Antibes where, before him, the Hôtel du Cap had been
kept open through that dangerous season only for the Chinese
Ambassador, who could not be expected to understand that he
was endangering his health and the lives of his children. And all
this, given the nostalgia for the twenties which now afflicts a
sadder, wiser generation, has turned Gerald Murphy into a kind
of minor literary figure — a character in a novel everyone has

read but no one has yet written. Indeed, it is often asserted that Murphy was the model for Fitzgerald's Dick Diver in *Tender Is the Night,* if not the model for Fitzgerald himself. People who have never seen or even heard of a Murphy painting know all about that famous party he and his wife, Sara, gave on a barge upon the Seine. They talk about the Count de Beaumont's automotive ball and how Murphy got himself welded into a costume of stainless steel the afternoon before and how the night wore on. They even quote a darkly ambiguous saying attributed to Murphy which seems to justify a Fitzgerald universe: "Living well is the best revenge." But because they have yet to learn that Murphy was a painter, a very serious painter, they have had no occasion to consider the tone in which a phrase of this kind might be spoken.

To any artist, and to a painter above all, the best revenge upon life, or more precisely upon death, is not living either well or badly but creating works of art, and Gerald Murphy, whatever he may have said upon the subject, knew it. His life, though he and Sara lived as bravely and as gracefully as humans can, was far from constituting a revenge on anything. It was a deeply tragic life, a life which sometimes seemed intentionally tragic, as though an enemy had planned it. And those luncheons on the thick blue plates under the linden tree at the Villa America were not a compensation for the suffering but almost an aggravation. The Murphys had three children. They were beautiful children: Honoria, an Alice-in-Wonderland little girl who melted with tenderness for animals, particularly horses; Baoth, a golden boy with a laughing delight in the world; Patrick, a child with the grave intelligence of a grown man — "un monsieur," as Picasso put it, "qui est par hasard un enfant." At the end of the Paris decade Patrick developed tuberculosis,

and his father, then deeply committed to his art, dropped everything, took the family to Montana-Vermala in the Swiss Alps,
devoted himself, with Sara, to the struggle for the boy's life, and
seemed, for a few miraculous months, to have won it. But the
Great Depression followed, and the family business on which
Gerald's sister, his sister-in-law, and his own family were depend-
ent, began to founder; he had no choice but to put his work
aside again and devote himself as best he could to learning the
trade. "Merchant Prince" he called himself with a black Irish
grin.

It was then that Patrick fell ill again and had to be sent to
Saranac. Yet it was not Patrick but Baoth who died first. Baoth
was away at school. He was just sixteen. He died of spinal
meningitis. And two years later, when he too had turned sixteen, Patrick followed. There was a bleak, blank memorial service in an empty New York church — a service in which the
silences were like the confrontation with the Voice out of the
Whirlwind in the Book of Job — and then the three survivors
moved into an apartment near the family business (near also,
ironically enough, the Museum of Modern Art, which Gerald
passed in the mornings, turning his head away). There Gerald
took for himself a small bedroom, bare as a monk's cell, where
he seemed to close the door upon his life.

He was in his late forties. He never, so far as I know,
painted again. And yet his life as a painter had not ended. It
had, indeed, only just begun. His few paintings existed and
were beginning to make their existence felt. Several were ex-
hibited in galleries as far away as Texas. One was acquired, just
before Murphy died, by the Museum of Modern Art, the word
reaching him, thanks to Alfred Barr and René d'Harnoncourt,
while he could still understand what was being said to him. This

picture, *Wasp and Pear,* was later loaned to the Tate Gallery in London, where it was shown in an exhibition along with the *Watch* owned by the Dallas Museum of Fine Arts. And subsequently, even during the period of his irrelevant fame as a character in contemporary fiction, the canvases continued their labor of establishing Gerald Murphy as what he really was and always had been, a painter of his time.

But a painter of his time in a rather particular sense of that phrase. Certainly when the pictures were painted they were quite unlike the work appearing in dealers' windows along the Rue La Boétie. Murphy's greatest admiration at that period was Piero della Francesca, most scientific and precise of fifteenth-century painters, and his passion was not for the abstraction of experience but for experience itself, "the thing itself" — the "thing" so like "itself" that it would *become* its implications. David Cecil tells us that Philip of Spain spoke of the young Elizabeth, radiant on horseback in the London streets, as "full of incantation." Murphy would have borrowed the words. He painted an Edwardian cigar box so totally representative of itself that it became its world. He painted a wasp so like a wasp that no one looking at it could take a wasp for granted ever again.

Toward the end of his life Murphy began to teach himself poems as he shaved. There was always a poem by the mirror, and it was always the work of the same man, Gerard Manley Hopkins. But it was never a poem chosen for that mastery of rhythms, that mysterious management of the English tongue, which brings later poets back and back to Hopkins' work. On the contrary, Murphy's choices were made for those images within the images, those images *of* the images, with which Hopkins' work abounds. In Hopkins too the world is "full of incantation."

3

President Johnson Alive and Carl
Sandburg Dead

BACK IN THE NINETEEN THIRTIES Carl Sandburg published
some lines in which he recorded the convictions of a Chicago
poet.

> One of the early Chicago poets,
> One of the slouching underslung Chicago poets,
> Having only the savvy God gave him,
> Lacking a gat, lacking brass knucks,
> Having one lead pencil to spare, wrote:
>
> "I am credulous about the destiny of man,
> and I believe more than I can ever prove
> of the future of the human race
> and the importance of illusions . . ."

No one who knew Sandburg would identify this as a self-por-
trait. Sandburg, though he sometimes slouched, was never underslung. There are, however, likenesses: traits and associations

in common. There was Chicago — even, one might say from here, early Chicago. There was that one lead pencil to spare. And there was, more obviously, the talk. Some will hear Sandburg's living voice, as I do, in "the importance of illusions." But the principal likeness, of course, is in the credo itself. Sandburg too was credulous about the destiny of man and believed more than he could ever prove of the future of the human race. Indeed it was precisely because he so believed and was thus credulous that he became the poet whose death has brought us here this afternoon — here not only to Washington but to this particular place in Washington. For this particular place is also committed to an unprovable and as yet unproved belief in the future of the human race; a credulity about the destiny of man.

Poets are not comparable. They are not, as the lawyers used to say, fungible, interchangeable like grains of wheat. You cannot measure one against another saying this one is larger or more durable than that one — "greater" as the textbooks put it. What foot-rule will measure the comparative dimensions of Walt Whitman and Emily Dickinson, of Sappho and Sophocles, of Dante and Donne? Poets, when they *are* poets, are as unique as poems are when they are actually poems: which is to say incomparably unique, essentially themselves.

But although poets can't be compared they can be distinguished. And one of the most elementary distinctions is that between the poet, however "great," whose achievement is in a particular poem or poems, and the poet, however incomparable, whose achievement is in the work as a whole, the body of the work, all sorts and kinds and degrees bound up together. Frost spoke unforgettably for the first when he said at a dinner in Amherst on his eightieth birthday that he hoped to leave behind "a few poems that will be hard to get rid of" — which, of course, he did — and more than a few — and far more than "hard to get rid of" . . . though perhaps nothing is really "more" than that. Sandburg might stand, in our own time at least, for the second. With Sandburg it is the body of the work that weighs, the sum of it, a whole quite literally greater than the total of its parts.

And what creates that whole, what binds the parts together, is, of course, precisely the credulity confessed by that slouching underslung Chicago poet. Sandburg had a *subject* — and the subject was belief in man. You find it everywhere. You find it announced in the title of the book in which his Chicago poet appears: *The People, Yes*. You find it in one form or another throughout the hundred-odd poems and proses of which that extraordinary book is composed. You find it in other poems. And in other books. Most important of all, you find it in the echo which all these poems and these books leave in the ear — your ear and the ears of others: the echo which has made the body of Sandburg's work a touchstone for two generations of readers — almost, by this time, for three.

A touchstone of what? A touchstone of America. If ever a man wrote for a particular people, however he may have reached in his heart for all people, it was Sandburg.

> *Between Amarilla and the North Pole*
> *is only a barb wire fence . . .*
>
> *Out here the only windbreak*
> *is the North Star.*

And if ever a man was heard by those he wrote for it was Carl. Europeans, even the nearest in that direction, the English, do not truly understand him but Americans do. There is a raciness in the writing, in the old, strict sense of the word "raciness": a tang, a liveliness, a pungency, which is native and natural to the American ear. And underneath the raciness, like the smell of earth under the vividness of rain, there is a seriousness which is native too — the kind of human, even mortal, seriousness you hear in Lincoln.

An American touchstone. But is there not a contradiction here? *Can* a body of work bound together by credulity constitute a touchstone for Americans? For Americans *now?* Once, perhaps, in the generation of Jefferson, or once again in the generation of Lincoln — but *now?* There is a notion around in great parts of the world — in Asia and in certain countries of Europe — that America has changed in recent years: that the last thing one can expect from America or from Americans today is credulity. It is asserted that the American people have now, as the saying goes, grown up. That they have put aside childish things, beliefs which can't be proved. That they have come to see what the world is, to put their trust in the certainties of power. That they have become, in brief, what is favorably known as "realistic": about themselves, about humanity, about the destiny of man.

Listening to contemporary speeches, reading the papers, one can see where these opinions of America may have come from. But are they true? Are they really true? Can we believe, in *this* place, thinking of *this* man, that they are true? Sandburg was an American. He was an American also of our time, of our generation. He died fifty-seven days ago. He was seen and known and talked to by many in this meeting. His struggles were the struggles of the generation to which most of us belong — the

130

struggles of the Great Depression and the many wars and the gathering racial crisis and all the rest. He was a man of our time who lived in our time, laughed at the jokes our time has laughed at, shed its tears. And yet *Sandburg was a credulous man* — a man credulous about humanity — a man who believed more than he could prove about humanity. And Sandburg, though he listened to those who thought themselves realists, though he was attentive to the hard-headed, was not convinced by them. In *The People, Yes* it is said:

> *The strong win against the weak.*
> *The strong lose against the stronger.*
> *And across the bitter years and the howling winters*
> *the deathless dream will be the stronger . . .*
>
> *Shall man always go on dog-eat-dog?*
> *Who says so?*
> *The stronger?*
> *And who is the stronger? . . .*

What Sandburg knew and said was what America knew from the beginning and said from the beginning and has not yet, no matter what is believed of her, forgotten how to say: that those who are credulous about the destiny of man, who believe more than they can prove of the future of the human race, will *make* that future, *shape* that destiny. This was his great achievement: that he found a new way in an incredulous and disbelieving and often cynical time to say what Americans have always known. And beyond that there was another and even greater achievement: that the people listened. They are listening still.

4

Eden in Hartford

❦

NOOK FARM (a "nook" means, among other things, a small parcel of land), began as a charming Hartford Eden on what was known in the eighteen sixties as the Hog River or the Meandering Swine. Its population, where it was not related to itself by blood or marriage — a tangled skein of Beechers and Hookers — was composed of congenial family friends: the Samuel Clemenses, the Charles Dudley Warners. Its doors were open. Its talk was lively. Its lawns were green. Its river was not yet polluted — though it was shortly to become what every river in the state soon was — an open sewer. Its music — at least when Mrs. Warner played — was admirable. And the general effect it produced on visitors from less fortunate cities — on one in particular from Hannibal, Missouri — was an effect of tranquility and peace and beauty. It was because of Nook Farm that Samuel Clemens decided Hartford was the best built and handsomest town he had ever seen. "They have the broadest, straightest streets in Hartford that ever led a sinner to destruction, and the dwelling houses are the amplest in size and the shapeliest and have the most capacious ornamental grounds around them." "Each house", he wrote, "sits in the midst of about an acre of green grass or flower beds or ornamental shrubbery guarded on all sides by the trimmed hedges of arbor-vitae and by files of huge forest trees that cast a shadow like a thundercloud . . . Everywhere the eye turns it is blessed with a vision of refreshing green. You do not know what beauty is if you have not been here."

And the same thing was true — substituting gas light for ornamental shrubs — of the life within. Not every inhabitant of Nook Farm could talk as well as Sam Clemens whose conversation, according to the Reverend Joe Twichell, had an "incomparable charm," but talk they all did and passionately and eagerly and well. Public affairs engrossed them, and there were few who were not crusaders for one cause or another: Abolition, or the Woman Question (pro and con), or the new Republican Party which even then had its liberal and reactionary wings, or the struggle for the right to speak one's mind. It was Nook Farm which, almost single-handed, supported Harriet Beecher Stowe when she dared to use the word "incest," in the *Atlantic Monthly* in an article on Byron — or, more precisely, on Lady Byron's memories of the private life of that uninhibited bard.

Thinking of Nook Farm as it must have been in its early days one has a twinge of nostalgia for an America which seemed about to realize itself and then, somehow, lost its courage: an America of an increasingly civilized, homogeneous, upper class of men and women — particularly women — who read widely, traveled frequently, talked well and kept their minds as open as their eyes — women who looked like the lovely Harmony Twichell and speculated as boldly, if not as oddly, as Isabella

Beecher Hooker and played the piano as brilliantly as Mrs. Charles Dudley Warner and spent their evenings, not, as their descendants do, at the bridge table or the television set, but in imaginative and often intelligent conversation which touched on everything under the heavens and a number of things presumably above them.

Some Nook Farm families were rich — though not, as the Clemenses demonstrate, permanently rich in the modern fashion: some, like the Stowes and the Hookers, had their seasons of lack if not actually of want. But none of them, though the great surge of affluence was beginning to fill and fall and fill again across the economy, were dominated by their possessions or lack of them as members of their American class were soon to be. Their minds were on different things: on ideas; on the realization of human hopes; on the struggle against slavery; on the recent theological revolution engineered largely by Horace Bushnell; on the religious skepticism of Mark Twain; even on the journey of General Hawley and his *Hartford Courant* from the extreme Republican left to the farthest Republican right . . . in brief on the whole perspective of the inquiring mind in those few exciting years at the end of the Civil War when the old walls seemed to be falling everywhere and the future — particularly the future as seen from Nook Farm — appeared as open as infinity.

And then, in 1872, the minds shut and the doors of Nook Farm with them. Henry Ward Beecher, the most famous preacher in the Republic and the brother of three Nook Farm women, was publicly accused of adultery with the wife of one of his parishioners in the Plymouth Church in Brooklyn, and while two of his sisters, Harriet Beecher Stowe and Mary

Beecher Perkins, defended his innocence, the third, Isabella Beecher Hooker, supported his accuser, her adored and dubious friend, Victoria Woodhull. Mrs. Hooker's motivation was not malicious: she loved Henry and Henry returned her affection, regarding her as closer to him than anyone else in the Beecher family. It was the theory of the thing that mattered. "Free love," meaning the freedom to love outside of marriage, was a new and exciting doctrine in those years and the beautiful Victoria Woodhull was its professor and its prophet. If Henry was guilty (and of course he was if Victoria said so) then the great issue was the issue of hypocrisy: he was practicing what he refused to preach, and Mrs. Hooker, though she was not sure she could accept the novel doctrine for herself, was determined to make an honest man of Henry. She never gave up. Even after the jury disagreed in the alienation suit and the court of eminent clergymen had "exonerated" their distinguished colleague, Isabella Beecher Hooker continued to hope for a confession. There is perhaps no sadder — certainly no stranger — scene in the intellectual history of America, than Isabella Beecher Hooker, waiting among the newspapermen for the deathbed confession and apology which she was sure was coming but which his family would not let her in to hear.

Nook Farm went on, of course. The houses were there and the shrubbery and, to some extent, the lawns. Mark Twain's house was alight after dark and full often of writers and convivial friends from distant parts — William Dean Howells down from Boston (his wife disapproved of Mr. Clemens' drawing-room manners), Bret Harte from the wilder west, Joel Chandler Harris from the south, Matthew Arnold from beyond the Atlantic, the marvelous Sarah Orne Jewett — but the old life was over. The worm had eaten the apple and the Gilded Age, which Mark Twain and Charles Dudley Warner had discovered under their noses and turned into a shaky novel, had thrown away the core. What was left of Nook Farm as the century ended, was what we see today — a few houses with memories of a better time.

That and one thing more — a text for sermons which might be relevant today. What had happened to the United States, and given Nook Farm its heady freedom a hundred years ago and more, was the breakdown — actually the dissolution — of the body of incontrovertible doctrine which had shaped the American community at its New England beginnings and held it rigidly together, first in fact and then in form, for two hundred years. The Beecher family, better perhaps than any other, illustrates the totality of the collapse. The Reverend Lyman Beecher of Litchfield, father of Harriet and Henry Ward and Isabella and all the rest, was like his forebears, an uncompromising Calvinist who believed, literally and unquestioningly, in the doctrine of infant damnation and all the rest of the iron dogmas. But his children, including his five preacher sons, had renounced Calvinism by the middle of the century — not only renounced it but, to all intents and purposes, stopped thinking about it. To Henry Ward Beecher, says one of his biographers, "the problem of evil had become almost trivial. Like his brothers and sisters he had shed the morbid doctrine of total depravity."

The result — and not for the Beechers alone — was the sense of release which produced the boundless optimism of that generation: its addiction to "causes" of every kind from spiritism to woman suffrage and on out to the abolition of sexual hypocrisy

136

and the freedom to sleep where you pleased. The phenomenon is familiar enough in human history and particularly familiar to us. It is when outworn structures of belief disintegrate that hope for a different, better world runs highest — and takes its most irrational forms. We have not, of course, discarded religious orthodoxy in this century: we had no religious orthodoxy left to discard. But we have done the best we could: we have discarded the social forms and conventions which took the place of religious orthodoxy when the Calvinist world came down. And the consequences have been much the same. We too — particularly the younger of us — have felt ourselves released. And released, like our predecessors of the nineteenth century, not into a larger freedom of the mind, but into a variety of eager "causes."

Spiritism is no longer fashionable and women's suffrage has already been attained — thanks not least to Isabella Beecher Hooker — but sex remains: remains, proliferates, and multiplies. Ours, I should guess, is the first generation since the plucking of the apple to which sex is no longer something natural (and lovely) to be accepted for itself but something theoretical and symbolic to be talked about for the sake of talking. Certainly we are the first generation since the printing press to produce a school of writers whose purpose is not to write but to put words on paper — words which earlier writers did not care to put on paper. And the same thing is true of politics. If sex has become a "cause" so has revolution. What was once a means — often a noble means — to attain an essential human end has become a fad, an intellectual obsession. Act first and find out later why you acted. Follow Che Guevara and find out where Bolivia is when you get there.

And other things as well have turned to "causes" now the rules of conduct are repealed. Even individual freedom has become a "cause" — and turned to irresponsibility. Where once it was the free man's business to be sure that other men were also free, now it is the free man's passion to be let alone — to live away from neighbors whose complexions might distress him — to wash his hands of suffering which is not his own — to hire more policemen and forget the rest, forget the others — and the country.

What Nook Farm might suggest to all of us is this: that the liberated generations, the generations born at the breaking down of walls, are not the most fortunate generations though they may be the most interesting, and even the most charming. No society can live without intellectual and moral order, and the fact that order decays with time like everything else merely means that order must be recreated with time. But order cannot be recreated by the pursuit of causes however grandiose and whatever they call themselves — love, liberty, revolution. Only justice and the love of man can produce an order that humanity will accept. It was the tragedy of the generation of Nook Farm not only here but throughout the United States, that it left the new and needed order to produce itself — which meant, in practice, that it left it to another generation to produce and all but shattered the Republic in the process. If we can learn that lesson from those trees and houses they will have served a purpose even Isabella Beecher Hooker would approve.

5

Mark Van Doren

❧

MARIANNE MOORE, in her precise and exquisite prose, asked difficult questions. "Must a man," she said, "be good to write good poetry?"

I say it is a difficult question. I mean it is difficult for us, not for Marianne Moore. Ours is a generation, a muddle of generations, which the word "good" embarrasses. We have told ourselves for the better part of a century that goodness is irrelevant to the rapidly changing world we live in. And even now that Watergate has taught us better we continue to insist that, in any case, goodness is irrelevant to the practice of an art. The implication of Marianne Moore's question, the implication that a man might be a bad poet because he is a bad man — because he is vain, vicious, perverted, dishonest, even vile — is, we say, no longer thinkable. Literally no longer thinkable. We are beyond all that. Humanity is beyond it. Poetry above all is beyond it.

But Marianne Moore with her candid and beautiful precision was not beyond it. "Must a man be good to write good poetry?" Her answer was: Probably. "Rectitude," she said, "has a ring that is implicative." "With no integrity," she said, "a man is not likely to write the kind of book I read."

I repeat these words not because they dispose of the question or make the unthinkable thinkable: current criticism has yet to catch up with them. I repeat them because they make it possible to talk seriously and honestly of Mark Van Doren now he is dead.

Mark Van Doren was first and foremost and above all a good man, a man famous in his generation for his goodness, for his decency, for his rectitude. He was also a poet. But it would be a delusion to suppose, as the fashion requires, that his goodness was irrelevant to his poetry. On the contrary it was the quality of his goodness which made his poetry possible, as the most superficial reading of his poems will demonstrate. And the same thing is true the other way around. It was true of Mark Van Doren, as it was true of Emerson and Thoreau, that it was his poems which gave him his particular *kind* of goodness.

To take the poetry and the goodness apart, therefore, would leave little honest or serious to say about Mark Van Doren. He would become, as so many poets do in the current vocabulary, a merely literary figure, a paper man, a man interesting because he had written and read. It is true that Mark Van Doren had written: many books, most of them memorable. It is true too that he had read: he was, I suppose, the best-read poet of the century — at least in his own language. But to stop there would be to miss the whole point of his reading and writing. He read and wrote not for the sake of literature but for the sake of life -- to learn life and live it as the men of Lorenzo's time had done and of Elizabeth's and, in this Republic, of Jefferson's. He read and wrote to *be*. To be what he, indeed, became.

Mark Van Doren

What did he become? For one thing, the great teacher of his generation. Not because he had read and was learnéd but because he had read and had learned. The subject of his famous course at Columbia was not Shakespeare reflected in the triple glass of erudition but Shakespeare lived in a man's life. Which is why his students remembered that course when everything else was forgotten. To have read Shakespeare with Mark Van Doren must have been something like talking of Shakespeare with John Keats. To Keats, too, Shakespeare was someone he had just now left along the road.

But, great teacher though he was, it is the poet we have to do with here because the poet was the man and bore the vision and the vision is what matters in the end. Mark Van Doren's vision of the world was not a literary vision, a vision so divorced from the human need for seeing that it bears no witness, can be true or false or anything so long as it conforms to the demands of letters. He never accepted the dark night of the soul which has been a standard literary property for so many dwindling years. His vision was a vision of death *and* life: of death as the end of life and life as the meaning of death.

A vision like that takes courage. Courage and love. The courage to believe in life and live it. The love that, having lived it, still believes. It takes a good man and a brave one — a man whose goodness can indeed make poetry, a man whose poems are the image of his goodness — to write a poem in this century like Mark Van Doren's poem which begins "O world, my friend, my foe . . ."

O world, my friend, my foe,
My deep dark stranger, doubtless

Unthinkable to know;
My many and my one,
Created when I was and doomed to go
Back into the same sun;

O world, my thought's despair,
My heart's companion, made by love
So intimate, so fair
Stay with me till I die . . .

O air,
O stillness, O great sky.

6

New England's Frost and Frost's New England

F ROST'S IS a curious situation. Dead a dozen years he remains
something of an enigma to his readers and even to the biogra-
pher he himself selected to explain himself to his posterity. Not
that Frost's achievement is in doubt. There is no question whatever of his achievement. He was a poet not only of his time but
of his tongue: one of the very few who deserve that designation. He was also a respected man of letters, one of the most
respected of his generation in this country. He was a lecturer
seen and heard and listened to from one coast of this continent to
the other. He was a public figure, an American symbol, who
appeared as such at the inauguration of a President. His manuscripts, autographs, memorabilia are preserved in the most distinguished libraries. He had, and has, readers everywhere on
earth. His poems, many of them, are known by heart to thousands and repeated over and over. But who the speaker in those
poems *is* remains a question not only to intellectuals and academ-
ics, who live by putting questions to the past, but to children in

schools who are given poems of Frost's to read at an early age, and to young men and young women who read them for themselves, and even to the old among their books. What does he mean? says the child. Who'd say a thing like that? says the young woman. I don't know, says the old man: I don't quite know him.

The answers aren't always easy, particularly if you start with the assumption, as most of us do, that you know them in advance. Who is the speaker in these poems? A Yankee, you say. What is he talking? Yankee talk. Isn't Frost down in quotes in the *Encyclopedia Britannica* as "the poet of New England?" Didn't he live and farm in Derry, New Hampshire? Didn't he write *North of Boston*? And of course he did. But the trouble is that if you start with the assumption that Frost was a Yankee poet you will expect him to write like a Yankee (which he often, but not always, does) and you will expect his poems to be New England poems, poems not only of the New England scene but of the New England mind, which they may not be at all. And it is there, at that point that you get the children's questions and the occasional uneasiness in college classes and the discomfiture of distinguished scholars who, having used Frost's predecessors among New England poets as keys to his work, have ended up trying to explain why the keys don't fit.

Take, for example, the famous ironic tone which pervades Frost's work. His poems, even the early poems given to children to read, echo with irony. Irony, of course, is a common Yankee device. But is Frost's irony Yankee irony? Try the edge on your thumb. The Yankee mind is ironic in the old Greek sense: it "dissembles" by saying more or less (usually less) than it means, and there is a laugh in the grain of the words to warn you. Frost's irony is something else. It is disturbing in its implications — tragic even — and it can be savage. (Read "Provide, Provide" again.) The difference is not in the humor or lack of it: there is enough humor in Frost for seven poets. The difference is in the irony itself, the *way* it mocks at things. And in the tone it imparts to the voice, the sense it gives you of the speaker.

Which means that the children are right. There is indeed a kind of contradiction in certain poems of Frost's if you read them in the assumption that they are Yankee poems. But it does not follow that the difficulty is in the poems. It is the assumption that needs to be reconsidered. And I can think of no better way to reconsider it than to look long and hard at New England with poems of Frost's, or fragments of poems, in your mind as you look. Do these words come out of that field, this pasture, those far trees, or is there a different relationship between the poem and the country? Is it the feel, the sense, the character of a corner of the continent that speaks in these lines? Or is it the other way around? Is it the man who sees that countryside, the man who loves it, uses it, employs it for his purposes that speaks to us — but speaks for his sole self?

I think there is no question but that it is the man who speaks — a sole and single man, a singular man, a uniquely singular man. I think that it is a mistake, to look for the New England mind in Frost's work or the New England feel. It was not New England that produced Robert Frost: it was Robert Frost who chose New England. And the relation of Frost to New England was not the relation of the native son, who can take his country-earth for granted, but of the stranger who falls in love with a land and makes (literally *makes*) his life in it.

Frost knew all that as well as we do. One of his most famous poems is a poem of that choice. The road "less traveled by" in "The Road Not Taken" is not, as teachers sometimes tell, the art of poetry. No road has been traveled longer than the art of poetry. The road "less traveled by" is the *way to* the art of poetry — the way Frost elected at the age of twenty-six when he moved into New England, real New England, country New England, to try to support himself and his family on a little farm in New Hampshire while he struggled to master that art.

> *I shall be telling this with a sigh*
> *Somewhere ages and ages hence:*
> *Two roads diverged in a wood and I —*
> *I took the one less traveled by,*
> *And that has made all the difference.*

He was neither the first, of course, nor would he be the last, to make that choice, take that impossible risk. Young writers, young artists, everywhere take chances. They bet their lives as men on their hopes as writers. They close their eyes to the odds, carrying their young wives with them — even children. But Frost was bolder than most, not only because the risk is greater in farming, particularly New England farming, but because he was less prepared to take it. He was city born and bred. He knew next to nothing of farming. And his knowledge of New England, real New England, was almost as thin.

His father had been a New Englander by birth, but not, as he frequently told his son and anyone else who could listen, a New Englander by choice. He was a Copperhead even as a child, and at sixteen he had run away from home in Lawrence, Massachusetts, to try to enlist in the Confederate Army. (He got as far as Philadelphia.) Robert himself was born in San Francisco of a Scottish mother from Leith, near Edinburgh, and San Francisco was his home for the first eleven years of his life until his father died and the broken family returned to Lawrence. And Lawrence, of course, was a thriving, industrial city which was *in* a New England countryside but not of it. So that Frost, when he bought his New Hampshire farm, was hardly a Yankee at all in the country sense.

And yet, *when* he bought his farm and got safely through his first winter . . .

> *How the cold creeps as the fire dies at length —*
> *How drifts are piled,*
> *Dooryard and road ungraded,*
> *Till even the comforting barn grows far away,*
> *And my heart owns a doubt*
> *Whether 'tis in us to rise with day*
> *And save ourselves unaided.*

. . . when he got safely through the first winter and settled down to writing, his poems became Yankee poems — became famous shortly as *the* Yankee poems of his generation. And it is there, precisely, in that curious, almost paradoxical, fact, that one finds the real key to his relation with New England.

Most of the American youngsters who, before and since, have taken the "road less traveled by," have treated their means of livelihood as means only. The farm, if they farmed, was a way of earning time to write, and the land they worked was just that — land. Not so Robert Frost. From the very first, as we can see in the earliest New Hampshire poems, New Hampshire was more than a means. It was a presence in the written word as well as in the farmland labor. New England became an all-including metaphor for everything Frost learned and came to feel a bee-tree for the honeycombs he was constructing. In the work of most poets, particularly young poets, you will find that themes change and scenes change from poem to poem, worlds change from book to book. As you read through Frost's first poems you are always "there": always in New England or what becomes, for the poem's purposes, New England. Where the early poems of most others owe the place where they were written merely for their bed and board, Frost's owe New England for themselves.

Take the first lines in the first poem (after the Epigraph) in his *Collected Poems*.

> One of my wishes is that those dark trees,
> So old and firm they scarcely show the breeze,
> Were not, as 'twere, the merest mask of gloom,
> But stretched away unto the edge of doom.
>
> I should not be withheld but that some day
> Into their vastness I should steal away . . .

It is not a particularly good poem — young, uneven, and awkward — but it shows you at once how Frost is using a characteristic New England scene; that view across open pasture toward the line of trees which ends the open everywhere in Massachusetts or New Hampshire or Vermont. At first "the merest mask of gloom," the trees become in his wish the "edge of doom," or a dark, unending "vastness" in which a man who wanted to might lose himself. And Frost, or so he says, was such a man: "I should not be withheld . . ." The longing for the dark, in other words, was in himself: he calls the poem "Into My Own." But the image which contains that longing is a New England image. And the man at the pasture's edge on one side, the trees against the sky at the other, compose the poem between them.

The same is true of other deeply private emotions, as for example the fear he speaks of in the winter poem I have quoted above. He called it "Storm Fear" and began it on a comic-apprehensive note appropriate to the city-bred in the silence and isolation of the country as the wind goes east and the snow begins:

> *When the wind works against us in the dark,*
> *And pelts with snow*
> *The lower chamber window on the east,*
> *And whispers with a sort of stifled bark,*
> *The beast,*
> *"Come out! Come out!"* —
> *It costs no inward struggle not to go, . . .*

But though the tone is light the fear is not only comic. There is an ancient human terror in that "stifled bark" and though "the beast" is a Halloween monster there is nevertheless something truly monstrous there — something that could scarcely have been confessed if New England, with its myths of winter, had not made the image possible. One thinks, reading this early poem, of a later and far greater poem which also begins with New England snow —

> *Snow falling and night falling fast, oh, fast*

and which ends, as this does, with a lightly spoken, an ironic
dread — but one which chills the heart.

> *They cannot scare me with their empty spaces*
> *Between stars — on stars where no human race is.*
> *I have it in me so much nearer home*
> *To scare myself with my own desert places.*

These obviously are not country poems in the usual sense —
certainly not pastoral poems. What they have to say about
country things — snow storms, scything, meadow flowers —
turns out to be something very different: something about man,
about the experience of being human, being alive upon this little
sun-struck, wind-worn planet . . . which will also end.

And the same thing is true of their New Englandness. They
are New England poems, yes — none more so — but not in a
descriptive or a geographic sense. They are New England
poems because the look and feel and smell of things in New
England is so profoundly and yet so intimately human: because
this landscape lets the human meaning through; because the
human asking is reflected here as nowhere else I know on earth.
What's on our minds as we read them is ourselves; our condition as men; our consciousness as human beings.

So what, then, is the answer to our question? What *is* this
ironic voice saying to us? This sometimes cruelly ironic voice,
what does it want with us? With our children? With that
young girl at the eager beginning of her life? Our *selves?* Well,
Frost left us an answer of sorts: a little poem he placed as epigraph at the beginning of his *Collected Poems.* It is called "The
Pasture," a word which always evokes New England for me,

and it is written in the teasing, tender voice a man might use to a
child — or to a woman he loved:

> *I'm going out to clean the pasture spring;*
> *I'll only stop to rake the leaves away*
> *(And wait to watch the water clear, I may)*
> *I sha'n't be gone long. — You come too.*

> *I'm going out to fetch the little calf*
> *That's standing by the mother. It's so young*
> *It totters when she licks it with her tongue.*
> *I sha'n't be gone long. — You come too.*

This is a promise, of course, writer to reader: come with me
and I will show you . . . What? A newborn calf? The water
clearing in a roiled-up spring? Frost has a word about that, too,
and in the same place, at the beginning of his *Collected Poems*.
It is a prose word and, like most of his prose, far less lucid than
his verse, but it is obviously meant — deeply meant. "The
figure a poem makes," he says, "begins in delight and ends in
wisdom . . . ends in a clarification of life . . . not necessarily
a great clarification," but at least "a momentary stay against
confusion." The words that catch our attention here are "wisdom" and its modifier, "clarification." What is the "wisdom"
in which the figure of a poem ends? Is he thinking of those
aphorisms, precepts, which are found so frequently in his early
poems? — "Something there is that doesn't love a wall?" "Men
work together/Whether they work together or apart?" There is
a poem called "Take Something like a Star," one of his "After-
words," which jeers at precepts:

O Star (the fairest one in sight) . . .
Say something to us we can learn
By heart and when alone repeat.
Say something! . . .

To which the star replies: "I burn." But the speaker persists in an urgent parody of the kind of question science puts to the universe:

. . . say with what degree of heat.
Talk Fahrenheit, talk Centigrade.
Use language we can comprehend.
Tell us what elements you blend.
It gives us strangely little aid
But does tell something in the end.

The star has no answer, of course, to talk like that but the speaker does. And the answer is not a maxim, "something . . . we can learn / By heart and when alone repeat." The answer is the star itself: a reminder that, when carried away, "We may take something like a star / To stay our minds on and be staid."

A diminished claim for "the figure a poem makes"? On the contrary a far bolder claim. To show a star — really to *show* a star (or a gentian, or a maple tree or the clearing water of a spring) so that the mind may confront it and the heart contain it, is immeasurably more difficult, more daring, than to compose an epigram, even a wise one. It is, indeed, the most difficult task on earth: the task of art.

What Frost is saying to those children who understand him but not quite, to the young who catch the irony behind the saying and resent it, to the old man winding up his thought, is what all art says: See! (Not *Look*, but *See*.) Anything can make us look, any chance movement in a room, the wind in poplar leaves, a paper bag uncrumpling in the sun. Only art can make us see. Henry Thoreau put the distinction as simply as it can be put in that amazing *Journal:* "There is no power to see in the eye itself any more than in any other jelly. . . . We cannot see anything until we are possessed with the idea of it, take it into our heads, and then we can hardly see anything else." It is true of the roiled-up water in that spring of Robert Frost's. And it is true too of his collected poems, take them all in all. They too perform the promise of the epigraph at the beginning: they *show*. We see because of them . . . and not New England only but the landscape of our hearts. As for the irony, irony too is a way of saying so that one may see: a reflection, a re-fraction, of the light that makes the too familiar visible.

Acknowledgments

Various sections of this book have appeared in other publications. "Bubble of Blue Air" was originally published under the title "Riders on Earth Together, Brothers in Eternal Cold" in the *New York Times*, December 25, 1968; © 1968 by The New York Times Company; reprinted by permission. Portions of "Return from the Excursion" were originally published under the title "Heaven and Earth and the Cage of Form" in the January–February 1968 issue of the *Rockefeller University Review;* copyright © 1968 by the Rockefeller University Press. "The Revolt of the Diminished Man" was originally published in the June 3, 1969, issue of the *Saturday Review.* "Master of Man" was originally published under the title "Great American Frustration" in the July 9, 1968, issue of the *Saturday Review.*

"The Premise at the Center" was originally published under the title "The Premise of Meaning" in the June 5, 1972, issue of *The American Scholar.* "News from the Horse and Wagon" was originally published under the title "Rediscovering the Simple Life" in the April 1972 issue of *McCall's.* "The Ghost of Thomas Jefferson" was first published under the title "Now Let Us Address the Main Question: Bicentennial of *What?*" in the *New York Times*, July 3, 1976; © 1976 by The New York Times Company; reprinted by permission. "Autobiographical Information" was originally presented as an address entitled "Conversation with the Moon" at the Cosmos Club in Washington, D.C. "Apologia" was first published in the June 1972 issue of *Harvard Law Review.* "Expatriates in Paris" was originally published under the title "There Was Something about the Twenties" in the December 27, 1966, issue of the *Saturday Review.* "A Lay Sermon for the Hill Towns" was origi-

ACKNOWLEDGMENTS

nally published under the title "The People Who Live Here" in the
February 1977 issue of *Yankee* magazine; copyright © 1977 by
Yankee, Inc. "The Venetian Grave" was originally published in the
January 26, 1974, issue of the *Saturday Review*.
"Gerald Murphy" was originally published as the foreword to the
Museum of Modern Art exhibition catalogue *The Paintings of
Gerald Murphy;* copyright © 1974 The Museum of Modern Art,
New York; reprinted by permission. "President Johnson Alive
and Carl Sandburg Dead" was originally presented as an address
delivered on the steps of the Lincoln Memorial, September 17, 1967,
and was first published under the title "Tribute to Carl Sandburg"
in the Winter 1968 issue of *The Massachusetts Review*. "Mark Van
Doren" was originally published in the Winter 1974 issue of
Daedalus; copyright © 1973 by The American Academy of Arts
and Sciences. "New England's Frost and Frost's New England"
was first published under the title "Robert Frost and New England"
in the April 1976 issue of *National Geographic;* copyright © 1976
National Geographic Society.

The author is grateful for permission to quote from the following
copyrighted sources. *Notebooks 1942–1951* by Albert Camus, translated from the French by Justin O'Brien; reproduced with permission of Alfred A. Knopf, Inc. *Complete Poems of Robert Frost*,
copyright 1942 by Robert Frost; reprinted by permission of Holt,
Rinehart and Winston, Inc. *The People, Yes* by Carl Sandburg, reprinted by permission of Harcourt, Brace, Jovanovich. *Collected
Poems of W. B. Yeats*, reprinted by permission of A. P. Watt & Son,
London. *Cántico: A Selection* by Jorge Guillén, edited by Norman
Thomas di Giovanni; reprinted by permission of Atlantic-Little,
Brown. *Collected Poems, 1924–1955* by George Seferis, translated,
edited and introduced by Edmund Keeley and Philip Sherrard; re-
printed by permission of Princeton University Press. *Seamarks* by
St. John Perse, translated by Wallace Fowlie, copyright 1958 by
Bollingen Foundation, New York. *Collected and New Poems:
1924–1963* by Mark Van Doren, copyright © 1963 by Mark Van
Doren; reprinted with the permission of Hill and Wang, Inc.

Index